Writers of Wales

Ben Bowen

Editors:

Meic Stephens

R. Brinley Jones

Advisory board:

Jane Aaron

Dafydd Johnston

Writers of Wales

Ben Bowen

T. Robin Chapman

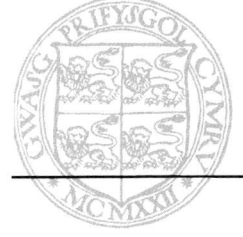

University of Wales Press

Cardiff 2003

© T. Robin Chapman, 2003

British Library Cataloguing-in-Publication Data.
A catalogue record for this book is available from the British Library.

ISBN 0–7083–1788–X

All rights reserved. No part of this book may be reproduced, stored in a retrieval system, or transmitted, in any form or by any means, electronic, mechanical, photocopying, recording or otherwise, without clearance from the University of Wales Press, 10 Columbus Walk, Brigantine Place, Cardiff, CF10 4UP. Website: www.wales.ac.uk/press

The right of T. Robin Chapman to be identified as author of this work has been asserted by him in accordance with the Copyright, Designs and Patents Act 1988.

Published with the financial support of the Arts Council of Wales

Typeset at University of Wales Press
Printed in Great Britain by Dinefwr Press, Llandybïe

Contents

Introduction 1
Chapter I 8
Chapter II 21
Chapter III 54
Epilogue 67
Bibliographical note 69
Index 71

Illustrations

All illustrations were first published in *Cofiant a Barddoniaeth Ben Bowen* (Caerdydd, 1904).

1. The unveiling of the Ben Bowen memorial, Treorci, August 1908.   4

2. Ben Bowen (left) aged 14, with father and younger brother Tom.   11

3. Ben Bowen (right), with fellow-students at University College Cardiff, 1900.   18

4. Ben Bowen in Kimberley, 1901.   41

5. Ben Bowen (left) with Dyfnallt at the National Eisteddfod in Bangor, 1902.   52

6. Ben Bowen's surviving brothers and sisters. David (Myfyr Hefin) stands far right; Mary is seated, left.   66

Introduction

WALES WITNESSED THE EARLY DEATHS OF THREE INFLUENTIAL FIGURES within twenty years of the turn of the twentieth century. Each of them subsequently enjoyed the kind of immortality that Edwardian sentiment liked to confer on what it considered to be unfulfilled greatness.

Thomas Edward Ellis (1859–99) was elected as Liberal MP for Merioneth in 1886. His victory represented the triumph of democratic radicalism over Tory squirearchy. For over a decade he articulated the Welsh Nonconformist agenda in a way which Lloyd George himself never quite achieved. He spoke passionately on land reform, secondary and university education and disestablishment and made numerous unsuccessful attempts to promote the setting up of a Welsh assembly. He reached the rank of chief whip in Gladstone's 1892 cabinet, was inevitably compromised by a conflict between party and personal loyalties, and died in Cannes where he had been sent by a friend to restore his poor health. He was buried at Cefnddwysarn, near Bala, and his statue now stands in the town's High Street.

A statue to Hedd Wyn (1887–1917) stands a few miles away at Trawsfynydd in the same county. A shepherd, self-taught poet and private with the Royal Welch Fusiliers, he fell at the battle of Pilkem Ridge in Flanders during the Great War. Six weeks later, his ode won the Birkenhead National Eisteddfod in 1917. The chair he had won was draped in a black cloth and left empty. His prizewinning piece, in a year when the composition was left open, was 'The Hero'.

Between these deaths, Ben Bowen died in 1903. He was twenty-four. A photograph, taken two years earlier in Kimberley, South Africa, where Ben was sent to recover, reveals as much as its studio formality conceals (see cover image). The subject's head is turned slightly away from the camera, throwing shadow across a scar on his right jaw caused in a mining accident when he was twelve. He would, it is said, unconsciously cover it with his hand in the company of strangers. Although the sepia cannot show it, the hair, smoothed and combed to hide its natural waves, is red. It had made him the butt of bullying during his schooldays. His forehead is broad, 'alarmingly domed', as one contemporary put it. J. Valant Williams, a phrenologist who had 'read' Bowen's skull in November 1898, pronounced it out of all proportion to his body, the head of an undoubted genius. His shirt collar sits loosely around his neck and his shoulders are round under an over-large jacket. At 5ft 7½ in., his weight at the time was somewhere around eight and a half stone. Tight lips cover a row of top teeth which were little more than stumps. He smiled seldom and reluctantly. Above all, though, one notices the eyes. They have an unnatural brightness about them, a sign of the tuberculosis which would eventually kill him. The photograph captures him, then, aged twenty-two, in the transition between a youth which had begun to win him a national reputation as a rising star and an adulthood which would test that early promise. The year which would ensure him an entry of almost a full column in the *Dictionary of Welsh Biography* was about to begin.

    This photograph was the image of which he was most proud. It conveyed at once the seriousness of the Baptist minister part of him still wished to become and the visionary poet he confidently believed himself already to be. He paid for two dozen copies at a cost of 30s. and posted them to friends, relatives and, above all, fellow poets who expressed an admiration for his work. It was the image that greeted the mourners at the memorial service, the photograph, too, which Ben's brother and literary executor, David (Myfyr Hefin), would use over the twenty-five years after his death as the frontispiece to most of the five volumes of his collected posthumous works. People who had never known him personally, and others who were not yet born when he died, grew up with it hanging in a black frame over the dresser or on a bedroom wall. With Ben dead, his photograph became an icon, a Nonconformist memento mori, a reminder that those whom the gods love die young.

For Myfyr Hefin, who lived on into the 1950s, Ben became virtually a cottage industry. Readers wishing to know more about the dead poet were referred to the Offices for the Work of Ben Bowen at 4 Hermon Street, Treorci. Between 1904, when he published *Cofiant a Barddoniaeth Ben Bowen* (The Biography and Poetry of Ben Bowen), and 1931 when, as editor of the Baptist magazine *Seren yr Ysgol Sul*, he included the last of his occasional series of selections from Ben's reading journal and pieces which might be attributable to him because they had been written in his hand, his brother's achievements obsessed him. Ben's sermons and other short pieces appeared as *Rhyddiaith Ben Bowen* (Ben Bowen's Prose, 1909), his juvenilia as *Blagur Awen Ben Bowen* (The Buds of Ben Bowen's Muse, 1915), the story of his last years was published in *Ben Bowen yn Neheudir Affrica* (Ben Bowen in South Africa, 1928), and in the same year a selection of the shortest and simplest 'Pieces of his work for Home and School' was compiled as *Ben Bowen i'r Ieuanc* (Ben Bowen for the Young). Profits from the biography, sold by subscription, raised the money to place a plaque on the house where he was born and erect a marble monument over his grave in 1908, a month before what would have been his thirtieth birthday. The sales of his other works endowed a scholarship in his name at Coleg Harlech, where his nephew, Ben Bowen Thomas, was warden.

The streets of Treorci were lined with mourners when he was buried on 20 August 1903. Despite torrential rain and high winds, thousands more packed the cemetery, among them the mayor of Cardiff. Of his legacy, his brother wrote:

> Welsh literature will be saturated for generations with tears of sorrow on his early grave, the path which leads to the place will be worn red by the feet of pilgrims for centuries, his grave will be doused with the

admiring tears of a numberless multitude as yet unborn, and Treorci Cemetery will be forever sacred to the Welsh nation as the place where the remains of Ben Bowen, the bard, rest. (*Rhyddiaith Ben Bowen*, p. ix)

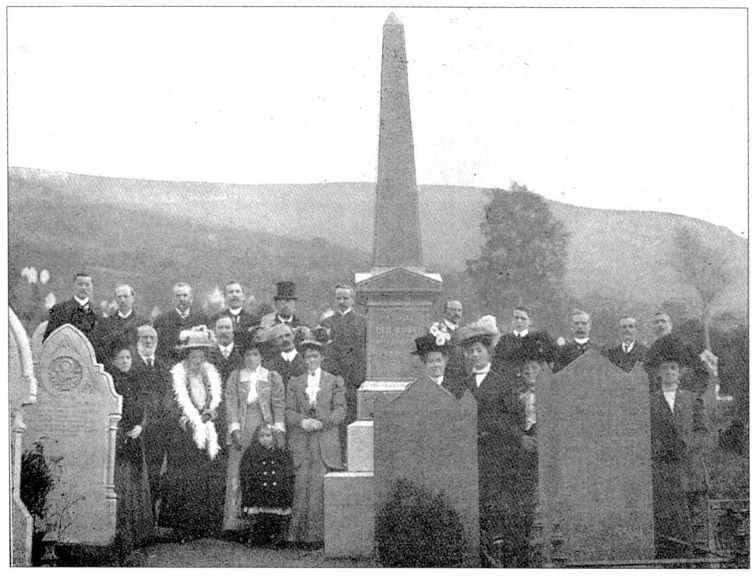

The unveiling of the Ben Bowen memorial, Treorci, August 1908.

Of the thousands who braved the storm that August afternoon, it is debatable whether more than one in twenty could have recited a single line of his work. Even though the 1901 census returns for the Rhondda show that 64 per cent of the population was Welsh-speaking, a number of them, no doubt, would have had only the vaguest understanding of the elevated language in which the proceedings were conducted. Ben Bowen's death coincided pretty closely with the beginning of the death of Welsh in the Rhondda Valley as a natural means of communication; his generation was arguably the last to speak it as a first language. Between 1901 and 1911, while the population of the Rhondda had grown from 103,740 to 139,335, the number of monoglot English had nearly doubled from 37,000 to over 60,000 and the number of those speaking only Welsh had halved. In 1903, reviewing the 1901 census returns for the numbers of Welsh-speakers across Wales, one correspondent in that embodiment of Welsh popular culture, O. M. Edwards's *Cymru*, urged his readers to draw a line from Newtown in the east to Llanelli in the west, discounting everywhere south of that line, including the Rhondda, as linguistic territory irredeemably lost. With the decline of Welsh came a corresponding fall in chapel attendance and the popular culture which centred on the chapels. By the time of the publication of the final two volumes which Myfyr Hefin was to edit, he would draw a distinction between the indifferent majority and the Welsh in the Rhondda who were keeping the memory of its famous son alive. By the inter-war years, the multitudes who would, Myfyr Hefin asserted, wear away the path to his grave and shed tears over this genius son of Wales had thinned to a trickle.

There are three dangers in any critical appraisal of Ben Bowen, relating to text and context alike. The first is to view his life and work solely through the lens of his early death. It makes much of his writing appear ironic when it is anything but. Irony exists in the breach between what the writer or character knows and what is known by the reader. Ben Bowen went through adulthood with the awareness that he would not live long. His poetic obsession with mortality was counterbalanced by a more mundane concern with the state of his own health. Like many late Victorians he was a believer in patent medicines, littering his letters home to Myfyr Hefin (which make up the bulk of *Ben Bowen yn Neheudir Affrica*) with reports on the efficacy or otherwise of Radam Microbe Killer, Owbridge's Lung Tonic, Congreve's Elixir and Sandow's Complete Developer. The irony, if it lies anywhere, lies in the unhappy coincidence of his own life's displaying so exactly what his audience saw as the *beau idéal* of a certain type of poet. Ben himself cultivated the image, comparing himself variously to Keats and to the legendary Golyddan, who had died aged twenty-two in 1862, leaving 40,000 lines of poetry.

The second and third pitfalls are the obverse of each another: either to take at face value the outpourings of his contemporaries, or – more likely, and more dangerously – to dismiss all the adulation as hot air. The tributes paid to Ben Bowen after his death were wordy and self-important, but they probably contained more genuine feeling than cynicism would have us allow. Moreover, the discourse of eulogy is revelatory. The tributes paid when the object dies young have a coherence which appears contradictory, even nonsensical. It was seen at its fullest in the display of grief which followed the death of Diana, Princess of Wales. The sorrow is at the same time public and private. The loss of the departed is deeply sad, but she has gone to a better place. Her death is mourned, but those who are left behind suffer more. She loved this world, but was too good for it. Her death is cruel, but a release; a crime, but fitting; dead but forever young. Victorian Wales explained the contradictions within a heaven/earth duality. Youth and talent combined, we are told, often prefigure death. An early death, therefore, is perversely a warrant of exceptional ability. It is to be welcomed as well as mourned because a prodigy who outlives his youth loses the elements that mark him as exceptional. Life saps it; death preserves it. In the words of Eluned Morgan, speaking at the unveiling of Ben Bowen's memorial in 1908 of a man she had met only for a few minutes: 'There is something lovely in the idea that he went home early, before the heat and labour of the day had taken the dew from the flowers of his life' (*RhBB*, p. xxvii). The prodigy in death is seen retrospectively as a visitor, living in this world but not entirely of it, his love of life the more intense because of an inner consciousness on his part that it will end before its due time. His true home is heaven. Another friend, Ifano Jones, again at the unveiling ceremony, said: 'It is easy to see and to remember – remember again the verdancy and brimful life of his stormy Spring, and think lovingly of him today developing and maturing in an eternal Summer.' His poetry is uncritically accepted as the work of genius because it is the work of a young man.

This monograph is, then, as much about the audience who lionized him while he lived and idolized him in death. What was the appeal of this mediocre poet of immoderate self-belief? More importantly, why was Ben Bowen, with his quick intelligence and facility with language, such a mediocre poet? A provisional answer to the second question will be useful here because it colours much of what will be said in the work that follows. Again the discourse of acclaim is significant. Ben Bowen has been seen as a restless soul trapped in a body which could not support it. It would be as true to say that his poetry was the product of an imagination trapped within a poetic and intellectual tradition which closed down the options for its expression. Although it is tempting to see Ben Bowen purely as a phenomenon, the object of his brother's uncritical esteem and of a more widespread morbid fascination, there are broader issues, too. His life and the reaction of others to it are snapshots of a mentality which was theological to a degree hardly comprehensible today, an aesthetic which equated abstraction with intellectual depth, a cult of youth every bit as strong as the cult of death which it parallelled, a measure of the ascendancy and vulnerability of eisteddfodic culture, the place of Wales within the British Empire and the industrialized south's place within Wales itself. Ben Bowen was born a Victorian and died an Edwardian. He lived long enough to see Wales and its literature change around him. The story of his life is the story of those far-reaching changes.

Chapter 1

Ben (not Benjamin) Bowen was born on 19 October 1878 at what is now 126 High Street, Treorci. Myfyr Hefin, probably as a challenge to prospective pilgrims – and partly, no doubt, because such a prosaic address would hardly fit the tale of heroism – would not state it directly: 'As you go up the valley from the direction of the bridge at Ty'nybedw Pit,' he wrote in the *Cofiant*, 'on the second street on the left – the street which leads downwards – and in the bottom house but three (which has now become a shop), Ben Bowen was born and raised' (*Cofiant a Barddoniaeth Ben Bowen*, p. x).

The Rhondda was in its economic heyday. It had overtaken Merthyr as the largest coal-producing area in Wales, its steam-coal production having increased by an estimated 450 per cent between 1865 and 1875. What had begun as a steady stream of migration from Montgomeryshire to the 'magnetic south' in the late 1860s had by the early 1870s become a flood from west Wales, swelled further towards the end of that decade by redundant steelworkers from Aberdare and surrounding areas. The population of the valley, 23,950 in 1871, had more than doubled to 55,632 by 1881, and that figure was set to double again over the following twenty years.

His parents, Thomas and Dinah, were natives of Carmarthenshire, part of the economic migration which by the last quarter of the nineteenth century had transformed the Rhondda into a chain of industrial villages. He was the seventh of nine children. His mother died when he was six. Ben Bowen, in an English essay written at the Treorci Board School in May 1897, said of his home town:

> Its heroes in literature, indeed, are scarce . . . It throws more life into Wales through physical labour than it does through mental labour. The coal trade is its only life-producing energy. Every other trade in it is but a derivative, direct or indirect. It lacks no more morals than any other district in the valley. The pages of its history are clean of a murderer's blood. It is crammed with privileges. It has a good library. It is full of life and joy, especially in the singing line. It has, indeed, a well-trained school, high in both morals and education, and possesses as joyful a set of children as any other district in the valley; and if they be noticed, they show its deep Welshiness [sic], which is the distinctive element in its character. Every child is a prophecy. Treorci's prophecy is 'Forward!' (*CBBB*, p. x)

They are the words of a young man who had recently left the pit himself, his style self-conscious in a way which never left him when writing in English. The content and order of the essay is, however, interesting: the emphasis on the area's lack of literary models, on its physical rather than mental energy, on ordinariness. It was no place for a man who felt himself called to self-improvement through education. The scramble for good things to say about the town – library, choir, school – seems a desperate *post hoc* attempt at mitigation. By the age of seventeen, Ben Bowen was already edging away from his roots.

His rejection of the Rhondda was, perhaps, a missed poetic opportunity, but he would have baulked at the idea of writing about his home. When he instructed Myfyr Hefin late in 1901, 'Open your eyes to what you are and to what your world is, and write about that, and you will receive more respect and praise for that than you will ever have for poetry about things too deep for you swim in', (*Ben Bowen yn Neheudir Affrica*, p. 82) there was no irony in his words. Ben Bowen knew that he could swim further and deeper than his prosaic brother.

He had gone to work in Ty'nybedw aged twelve, at his father's insistence. Myfyr Hefin recalls Ben being brought by an older miner to the seam where he and his father were working at the end of Ben's first day. He was in tears, begging to be allowed back to school. Family circumstances would not allow it. The

Cofiant makes great play of Ben's acceptance of his role. At the same time, it hints at a rebellion. Myfyr Hefin recalls that he determined 'to make a university of his home', and slips into the dramatic present to relate how Ben became a poet on the very evening he received his first wages:

> But what would Ben do with his first 'pocket money'? There is our father at the table counting the little money he had back and forth. 'And here's a shilling for you, Ben,' he said. Ben accepted the shilling with thanks, and straight away there goes Ben out of the house with the shilling still in his hand. There he goes across the main road, past the Red Cow which is near his home without taking any notice of it, and past a number of other shops. At last, he reaches the shop of that kind old bookseller, Davies Bryncethin, and he asks him whether he will sell him *Yr Ysgol Farddol* that evening – that he would bring the other shilling next Saturday. Anyone who knew the old bookseller knows that he wouldn't say no by refusing a book to any boy who is fond of reading. Should not behaviour so full of love be a lesson to the booksellers of our country, and to our young boys? And that was Ben's custom for as long as he worked – a new book every Saturday wages night as a rule. (*CBBB*, pp. xiv–xv)

Yr Ysgol Farddol, Dafydd Morganwg's 1869 handbook of approved *cynghanedd* metres for strict-metre poetry, became a source of fascination. By thirteen, Ben Bowen had mastered the *englyn*, a four-line stanza with internal rhyme, assonance and alliteration. By fourteen, he had a grasp of the full twenty-four metres. At sixteen, he composed an elegiac ode to his cousin. His talent, like that of countless other would-be poets before him, was to serve an apprenticeship, to learn technique, to command the means of poetic production without necessarily having anything particular to say. His subjects would be dictated by the demands of local eisteddfod competitions: an *englyn* on 'The Blacksmith's Hammer', for example, or an elegy to departed worthies. It was not necessary to have known the subject personally; the eisteddfod secretary would provide biographical information to entrants on request.

Ben Bowen's whole career as a poet, and later as a preacher,

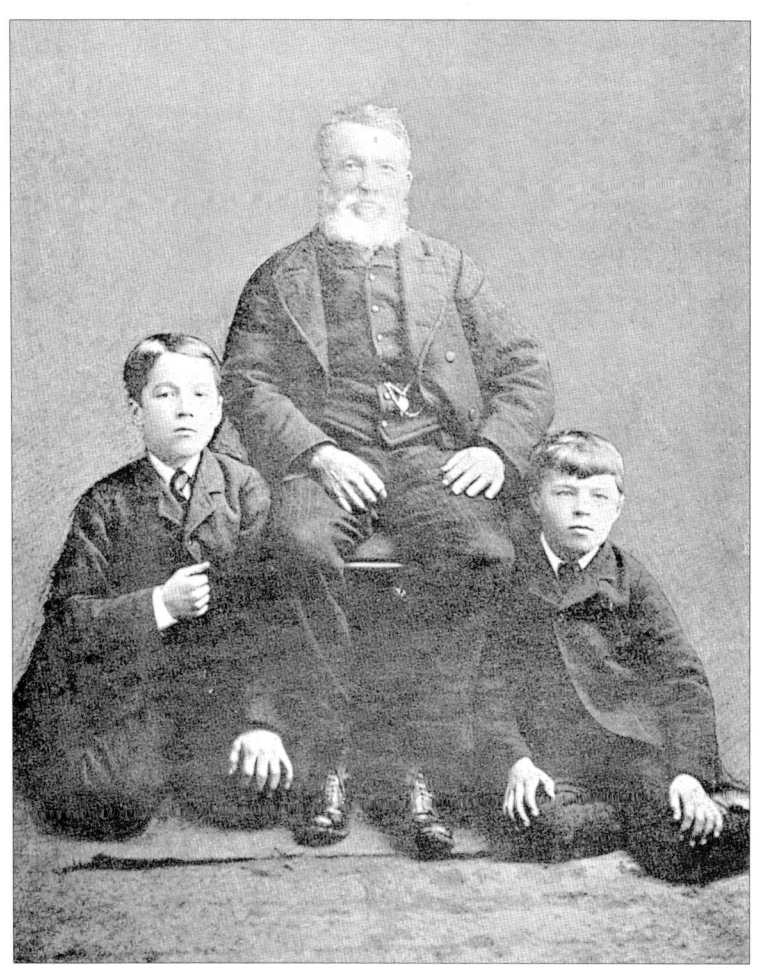

Ben Bowen (left) aged 14, with father and younger brother Tom.

would be governed by the principle of escape through self-improvement, the legitimization of ambition as service. For those who possessed a modicum of talent, a flair for self-publicity and a willingness to conform, poetic opportunities abounded. In a curious reversal of the system which had existed in medieval Wales, as the Victorian ruling classes became estranged from the Welsh language, the self-educated working classes assumed responsibility for literary patronage. The hierarchy was firmly in place by the time Ben Bowen took his first steps. Eisteddfod competitions (fifteen in the Rhondda Valley alone in 1899 and nineteen a year later) offered the chance to gain an audience and critical appraisal. Alongside these existed a support network of local papers and small presses (seven in the Rhondda by the 1880s) which were willing to satisfy a demand for popular work in Welsh, often through subscription. From what one critic has described as this 'tonnage of poetising', national magazines, in particular *Y Geninen*, published annual eisteddfod specials to bring local work to wider prominence. The summit, of course, was a National crown or chair.

By his early teens, then, Ben was both a miner and a poet. Myfyr Hefin, who worked alongside him, was stirred by the contrast: 'He climbed the hills of Parnassus from the depths of the coal mine, and lit stars of thoughts in that pitch-black darkness. He composed in chalk on a piece of slate nicknamed *y garreg farddol* – "the poet's stone"' (*CBBB*, pp. xv–xvi). The ideal of spiritual and academic self-improvement remained. He carried a pocket New Testament and an arithmetic primer.

It was at this time that he was baptized at Moriah Baptist chapel in Pentre, the village where he now worked. In the letter he later wrote to the theological college in Bangor where he hoped to train for the ministry, he attributed his conversion to 'some kind of growth, of which I can hardly give any account, but I have confidence in its reality'. Within months of his baptism he had become a Sunday school teacher. It would be unjust to attribute Ben Bowen's conversion to a less worthy motive, but in the context of late-Victorian Wales, the pulpit certainly represented another route to financial and educational opportunity, or at the very least a retreat from industrial drudgery. Nonconformism, like poetry, was as much a growth industry in the Rhondda as coal. Moriah chapel, where Bowen was received at the age of fifteen, was one of seven chapels opened in Treorci between 1867 and 1877, which between them had seating for 4,820 souls. His simultaneous attraction to poetry and chapel seemed the ideal route to becoming that uniquely Welsh hybrid, the *bardd-bregethwr* or preacher-poet. It coincided with his father's sudden paralysis, which left him unable to speak and incapable of work. Bowen remained at the pit. As the family's financial position became more strained, the desire to escape became more desperate.

After years of success in minor competitions, Ben Bowen's diligence and ambition were rewarded in October 1896, when he won the chair at the Penrhiw-ceibr eisteddfod, the youngest winner in the history of any eisteddfod competition. A second, more prestigious chair followed at Aberdare in February 1897 for a *pryddest* on 'Y Deffroad Cenedlaethol' (The National Awakening). O. M. Edwards, undisputed arbiter of popular Welsh taste, devoted two pages to the victory in his short-lived magazine, *Heddyw*, along with a request for financial support for the young poet to receive higher education. O.M. himself wrote in that May's issue:

> And since his talent is exceptional, and his circumstances pitiable, and his father unable to work for nearly three years because of paralysis, we would not wish to close the door in the face of whoever may be able to help. And which literature-loving heart cannot fail to feel for such a worthy cause[?] It is also worthy of note that he is a religious boy, and that there is no shadow of the follies of the older poets about him, – namely drink and futile games. He is very active with the Sunday School, and with everything that does good in the world.

Back home, on 20 February 1897, a celebration was held at Moriah. There was singing to the harp, a pianist and a singing party entertained, and the evening ended with no fewer than nine addresses by local worthies. For those who had missed the original, the company then re-enacted the chairing ceremony at Aberdare. The local paper, quoted in *Heddyw*, reported that when he was called to stand by his bardic name, 'Echo', 'a red-headed, grey-faced, quiet-looking, lad with a boyish appearance stood up and was escorted to the chair'. On the same evening a committee was formed to help Ben Bowen realize his talents. By late April in the same year, Ben Bowen had left the pit to return to his old school, intent on securing a place at Pontypridd Academy. His fees were met by a public concert held at the Drill Hall in Pentre which raised £47.

He spent the summer before taking his place in Pontypridd, in Monmouthshire, the furthest he had ever travelled from home. In a letter (in English) to his schoolmaster in Treorci he expressed 'a stir in the depths of my being, some strange and nameless feeling, at the quick-developing English tendency that reigns in sweeping force there. But I soon found my way out of it, or rather a way to forget it' (*CBBB*, p. xx). He visited the home of Islwyn, the mystic poet who had died a few months before Ben was born, and was allowed by the late poet's sister to sit in each of his bardic chairs in turn. Afterwards he went to visit his hero's grave, 'a beautiful red granite stone, that cleaves the air in a sharp, wedge-like manner' (Ibid.). In August he visited the National Eisteddfod in Newport, writing again to his old schoolmaster that the subject for the *pryddest*, 'Arthur y Ford Gron' (Arthur of the Round Table) had 'enough scope for the strongest poet in Wales to display his uttermost energy. He could make the nation's heart his own heart, throbbing with a life-giving pulse in this poem . . . an honour scarcely do we believe that one of our bards can claim' (Ibid., p. xxi). If Ben Bowen competed, he left no record.

That autumn he started at Pontypridd Academy, travelling each day by train from Treorci. He was to remain there for the next fifteen months. At his master's insistence, he devoted himself to writing short prose exercises in English – generally three hundred words or so in length – including the piece on Treorci quoted above. Their subject matter is trite, but they show a mind already willing to embrace contradictions, an advocate's passion to defend a position. 'Country Life' and 'The Advantages of Town Life', written within five days of each other in October 1897, for example, argue contrary cases with equal fervour: 'The sublimity of manhood grows from the simplicity of the country' (*RhBB*, pp. 223–4), says the first; 'Town life is the vital force of humanity' (Ibid., p. 226), counters the second. The topics are secondary: what matters are rhetorical flourishes, well-turned epigrams, a talent to appear wise. In 'Character', Bowen opines that 'Character is the most important thing in the world'. '"The Dog that Snapped the Shadow Dropped the Bone"' (Ibid., p. 225) informs us that 'Prudence is the soul of success' and that 'The man who has no ideas needs no whims'. 'Little Birds of Spring', dated 1897 but without a month, is no more than a string of such neat little sophistries:

> Spring is the king-maker of the year, and youth the king-maker of life. Spring is a prophecy that hath its fulfilment in after days. Youth is a dream that sometime somewhere finds its reality. Neither of them is made by days, but by joys. An old man in days and in experience may be young in dreams and joys. What dreams are to youth, the warblings of birds are to Spring.
> How pitiful it is to see a new-born babe on the bosom of a dying mother. However strange it may appear, it is so with Spring and Winter. Spring is born in a breeze. Winter at the same moment dies in a storm. Spring burst into rapture and song while Winter swoons in a dying groan. Spring's primrose, its banner of victory, is first planted on Winter's grave. The grave of one becomes the throne of the other . . . (Ibid., p. 221)

And so on. It all makes pretty tiresome reading. What Bowen had learned before he had reached his twenties, however, was the rhetorical power of setting up oppositions. This duality would find expression in his poetry, eventually becoming its essence.

In November 1897, he published the only work which carried his name during his lifetime: *Durtur y Deffro* (The Turtle Dove of the Awakening), a sixpenny volume containing his Aberdare *pryddest* and shorter pieces. It sold upwards of 1,500 copies inside a year, primarily through public subscription. At the beginning of 1898 in all likelihood, although the paper does not carry a date, Ben Bowen wrote:

MY DECISIONS

I. Not to be too at home away from home. To be wise.
II. Not to be talkative in company. To behave modestly. Humility is stronger than aggression.
III. Not to make the production of laughter an aim. That is the work of a fool.
IV. To seize every opportunity to read, and when in talkative company, to be quiet and thoughtful.
V. When a bad thought comes to disturb meditation, to think of the peace of Jesus. 'My peace I give you' – peace in the middle of sufferings – Jesus's life was peace – his sufferings were the giving of it. The persecution of this life is God giving the peace of heaven. There must be Winter before there is Summer; night before the dawn; a cloud before there is a rainbow; persecution and peace. The world giving persecution; Jesus giving peace.
VI. To make Jesus the King of life, the unseen guest at the table for every meal; and the Listener to my every conversation.

(*CBBB*, p. xxiii)

At the same time he began to preach, visiting Baptist churches throughout the Valleys. His sermons display a youthful impatience with orthodoxy, an attraction to non-literal interpretations of scripture, even a hint of pantheism. One senses here, too, the influence of those prose exercises at Pontypridd: the same concern with crafting oppositions and correspondences, a desire to deconstruct abstracts. The style is clipped and methodical, clever but passionless. The prose leaves no room for *hwyl* or religious abandon. The sermons are only incidentally devotional. In a Christmas sermon with Luke 2: 2 as its text, 'To you this day is born a Saviour . . .', Bowen logic-chops in a way which confuses the reader and must have utterly bamboozled his original congregation:

> A tiny child today knows that the world is a round ball. The idea many have today about life is similar to the ideas of our forefathers about the world. But life is not something long, broad and finite; but something round and infinite. The world is a world for life; and the life of the world is like the world of life – something round. One can make a voyage around the world and set off and end at the same place. The same place to set off and finish; and if necessary, make the same place the starting-point of another voyage . . . One life is the start of a journey, another life is the end of the journey of the first life, and that life in turn a starting-place for another life yet; and so on until God is reached. Then the One who was the beginning of all things shall be the end of all things – Alpha and Omega. A 'new start' is but another form of 'old end'; and 'old end' in changed clothes is a 'new start'. (*RhBB*, p. 15)

Another sermon, describing Jesus preaching to the crowds from a boat in Mark 2: 13, begins with this semantic preamble:

> There is change in development; but change is not development. A change is not always for the better, but for better and worse in as far as it is in itself. To change is not to improve, and failure to change is not to improve either . . . Change is proof of strength and not of weakness. Let us remember that the essence of development is change for the better. There must be a new strength in everything before it will grow . . . Development is a change in progress and to progress. A boy changes his opinion because he develops in intelligence. Change and development arm-in-arm support the arms of life. (Ibid., p. 63)

The sermons contain more substance than this, of course, and will be considered again in the context of Ben Bowen's later crisis of faith. But it is still fair to say that his early interest in language was determined by three factors: first, there was an adolescent interest in defining and compartmentalizing; second, he saw mastery of language as a means of rising above the social restrictions into which he had been born; and, third, language,

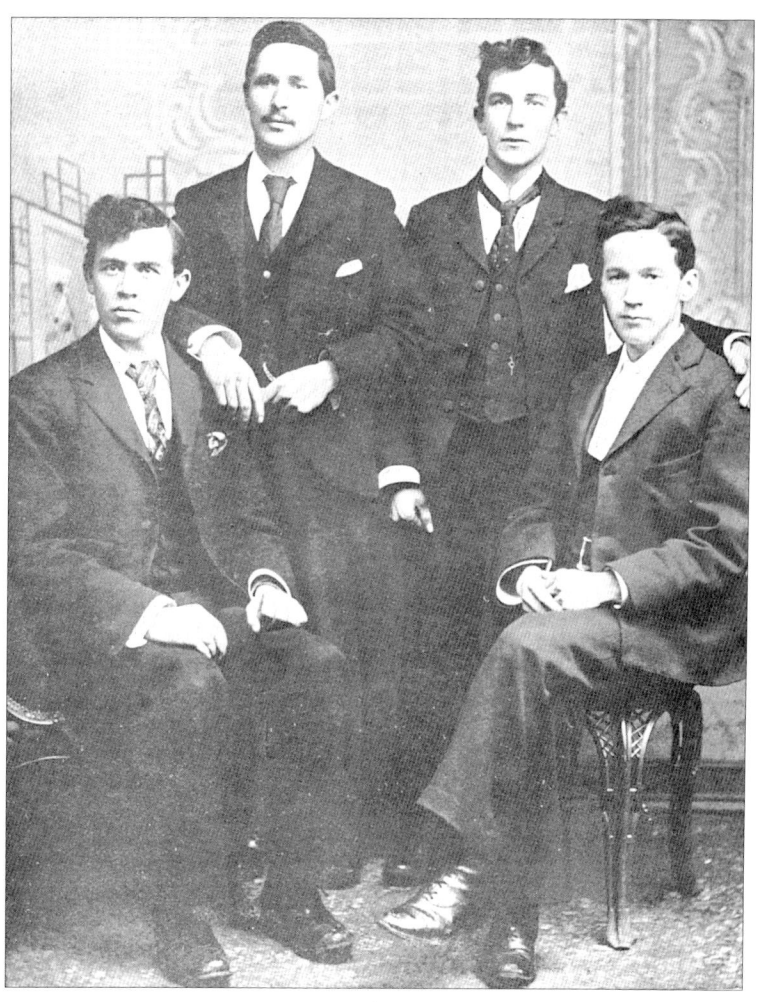

Ben Bowen (right), with fellow-students at University College Cardiff, 1900.

whether pulpit oratory, poetry or prose, provided a means for gaining attention and admiration.

His father died in October 1898. By January of the following year Ben Bowen had left Pontypridd to enrol as a student with the Cambridge Correspondence University, hoping to gain a general arts degree. His archive contains the material through which he worked in the early part of that year, from trigonometry to verse translations of Horace and Catullus. That summer, he failed the matriculation examination. A trip to Brymbo near Wrexham followed. It was in part a preaching tour, cut short by an unexpected haemorrhage. He returned home with no prospect of work, unable on medical advice to resit the Cambridge examination.

In January 1900, however, he felt well enough to leave Treorci for University College, Cardiff, lodging with a friend at Bangor Street in Roath while he prepared for a second matriculation paper. His health was poor. In May, he returned to the Rhondda, 'for good', as he wrote to a friend in Brymbo, to stay with a married sister, Mary, in Ton. 'The present stage of my career is very critical indeed. I am trying my best to get over it. If I fail I shall submit to my God, saying, "Thy will be done"' (*CBBB*, p. xxvii). He turned his attention to the *pryddest* competition for the 1900 National Eisteddfod in Liverpool, 'Williams Pantycelyn', writing in the introduction: 'Let him who wishes to criticize remember this – that the author completed his pryddest before he was twenty-one years old, and in very poor health – much of it when he was unable to leave his room' (Ibid.).

A rumour that he had won the crown persuaded him to make the journey to Liverpool that August, confident of victory. In the event, he was placed second. The Rhondda Cymmrodorion fêted him on his return, but Ben Bowen was unable to attend the meeting organized in his honour due to another haemorrhage. Another committee, this time under the auspices of the Cymmrodorion, organized a testimonial which succeeded in raising £350 in three months to send him to South Africa for his health. Reporting the scheme, the *South Wales News* described Ben

Bowen as 'a genius if ever there was one in these prosaic days in Wales' (Ibid., p. xxix).

By the end of the year a leaving celebration had been arranged at which his talents and good character were again praised and verses sung in his honour. Accepting the money, Ben Bowen said that his heart was too full to speak. 'If there had been a life of service behind it, he could understand it', the *Herald of Wales* reported him as saying, 'but it is being given for the sake of that which the future may bring about, which shows that there is in the tender heart of the Welshman much room for hope' (Ibid., p. xxxii). Presenting him with the money, his minister claimed to see the hand of Providence in Ben Bowen's departure, a divine plan to send him to work for God on a new continent.

On 26 January 1901, he sailed on the *Norman* from Southampton for Cape Town. 'I am leaving with an oratorio of prayers in my ears', he wrote to a friend. His brother compared Ben's departure with Arthur's retreat to Avalon to recover from his wounds. Bowen saw in it, too, echoes of Christ's retreat into the wilderness:

> Af yno i anialwch gwyw
> Am weledigaeth fad;
> A ddof yn ol yn broffwyd Duw
> A neges at fy ngwlad? (Ibid., p. 194)

> (I go into the withered desert
> For a splendid vision;
> Will I return as a prophet of God
> With a message for my country?)

Chapter II

THE YOUNG POET WHO SAILED FROM SOUTHAMPTON FOR CAPE TOWN IN January 1901 was a pure product of the nineteenth century. The man who returned to Wales in July the following year is less easily classifiable. By the time of his death he no doubt had some intimation of the direction Welsh poetry would take and, in his own clumsy way, he had played a part in its development. He was, however, constitutionally unable to embrace it with the enthusiasm he might. From the point of view of literary history, his death was convenient in that it never obliged him to do more than hint at an awareness that a new century demanded a new aesthetic; but at the same time it stifled a potential greater than even his most ardent admirers at the time may have guessed.

The story of the literary renaissance of the early twentieth century is well documented. Secular in tone and academic in approach, its driving force was praise poetry. At one extreme, W. J. Gruffydd and Silyn Roberts in *Telynegion* (Lyrics, 1900), sought to restore to Welsh poetry the simplicity of the pre-Revivalist folk lyric. At the other, most famously in T. Gwynn Jones's winning *awdl* at the 1902 Bangor Eisteddfod, 'Ymadawiad Arthur' (The Passing of Arthur), and R. Williams Parry's 'Yr Haf' (The Summer, 1910), it revelled in a pre-Raphaelite world of lavish escapism. The movement, though, owed more to medievalism than its subject matter and its recycling of arcane vocabulary. It was brought about in large measure, too, by the rediscovery that the genius of *cynghanedd* lies in a combination of craft and serendipity. As Dafydd ap Gwilym had done in the fourteenth century, Gwynn Jones, Williams Parry and other apprentices found that the strictures of the form could be perversely liberating. An aesthetic of happy accident could lay open associations of ideas which the poet might never have hit upon otherwise. Exigencies of rhyme, syllable, accent and a specified order of consonants could create a concept or image rather than merely govern it. The *cynghanedd* in Gwynn Jones's 'yn aeddfedrwydd lleddf hydref' ('in the wistful maturity of autumn'), for example, hinges upon the repetition in order of the consonants *dd*, *d*, *f* and *r* in a line of seven designated syllables. The adjective *lleddf*, therefore, is essential because no other meaningful monosyllable with the correct order of consonants exists. Its appropriateness is a fortunate coincidence. The repetition of fricatives enhances the gentleness of the description, and a secondary meaning of *lleddf*, used to distinguish minor from major keys in music, gives the line something akin to the quality of the opening bars of Elgar's cello concerto.

It was Ben Bowen's misfortune that he lived long enough to be aware of this renaissance, but did not have initially the temperament or later the opportunity to be fully a part of it. Had he been more alert to the influence of German lyricism, as, for instance, was John Morris-Jones, or had he developed the passion of Gwynn Jones and others for Middle Welsh prose, he might have been a better poet. He could never, though, have been a more popular one because the talent which won him praise while he lived and something bordering on veneration in death was his precocious ventriloquism. He was admired because he was a youth who in his poetry could do a more than passable imitation of a man twice his age. Other voices spoke through him.

The institution of the eisteddfod was, of course, significant. It established the accepted idiom for Welsh literature in an era without any other secular counterweight. Its aesthetic tended towards the declamatory and the grandiose. Moreover, its ceremonial and regalia – with its overtones of royal, academic and religious distinction – created a market of ambitious, competitive young men intent on displaying their talent in public, eager for the celebrity that a crown or chair would give, and motivated in no small part, too, by the desire for financial reward. In a puritanical era, the nineteenth-century eisteddfod offered a rare occasion for self-indulgence and innocent gossip. For Ben

Bowen, and hundreds like him, local and national eisteddfodau dictated the subject matter of their verse and its form. They guaranteed, too, an audience where it mattered for verse which could remain anonymous unless it was considered worthy.

Because of his dominance over eisteddfod culture at the time, the voice which spoke most strongly was that of the *Bardd Newydd* or New Poet. Whether this cabal of preacher-poets ever constituted a literary movement is debatable; but what one critic, Thomas Parry, has called their 'arucheledd llafurus' or 'laboured loftiness' was orthodoxy throughout virtually the whole of Bowen's short life. The *Bardd Newydd* was Nonconformist in upbringing, earnest by disposition and a crude Christian Platonist by design. He effected to inhabit a world which was merely a shadow of deeper, divine realities. Truth was reverenced and assiduously pursued, but never defined. Indeed, the poetry consisted – self-defeatingly – in stating how unknowable the universe was and how inadequate language was to express its eternal verities. Often, the most that a poet could do was to ask rhetorical questions or to proclaim his own ignorance as a warrant of the depth of his chosen subject matter. Elfed, for example, a poet with a talent for simple hymn-writing and unpretentious lyric verse in later life, wrote of the immutable law which governs the universe:

> Deddf, O Ddeddf! Y mae ei chylchdro mor ddiwyro ar ei chant
> Ag yw ergyd croyw'r seraff ar ryw hoff lesmeiriol dant;
> Mae y bydoedd ar ei braich yn syllu ym myw ei llygaid clir –
> Ar ei haeliau ni ddisgynodd cysgod cwsg trwy'r oesau hir.
> Croesodd drothwy tragwyddoldeb gyda 'Bydded' ysgafn-droed,
> Ac ni wyr pa beth yw oedran yn ôl arfer cyfrif oed:
> Ffurfafen ansigledig yw ei thabernacl hardd,
> Cerdda drwyddynt yn fyth ieuanc megis Efa yn yr ardd.

> (Law, Oh Law! Her circuit is as unswerving on its hub
> As is the melodic strum of the seraph upon some bewitching string;
> The worlds on her arm gaze into the depths of her clear eyes –
> The shadow of sleep has never fallen upon her eyelashes through
>   long ages.

She crossed the threshold of eternity with a light-footed 'Let It Be',
And she knows not what age is as it is commonly measured:
Her beautiful tabernacle is a changeless firmament,
She walks ever-youthful as Eve in the garden.)

For Bowen, the *Bardd Newydd*'s legacy was threefold. First, it prescribed the topics which were deemed appropriate; and, second, it clothed those same topics in a style which confused obscurity with dignity and took mangled syntax to be a guarantee of depth. Third, it shaped, too, the way in which the young Bowen perceived the natural world, looking not so much at nature as through it, treating it as a means of understanding divine will. 'The world is God's painting-room,' he wrote in an English essay in 1897, 'heaven his art gallery' (*RhBB*, p. 219). In a sermon later in the same year he expanded on the idea:

> Creation is God's painting-room, where he paints pictures to display on the walls of Heaven some day. The Holy Spirit is the artist. Providence is the finely wrought brush of Heaven. Mankind is God's canvas. It is only the paint which exists in the material world. Only on the curtains of the mind is the paint transformed into a living, thrilling picture. In the mind the order and beauty of the universe come into view, but they do not come into existence . . . Matter is life sleeping on the pillow of the infinite. (Ibid., p. 89)

In his poetry nature is, by extension, both an imperfect reflection of heavenly design and a means of interpreting that design. Things earthly do not merely serve as convenient metaphors for things divine: they are their counterparts, their shadows. Lilies are innocence, mountains magnificence, a storm at sea is a storm in the soul, sunrise the promise of life everlasting. What appear to be shop-soiled images are for Bowen literal truths. The drama of human suffering and redemption, doubt and faith, despair and assurance, is endlessly played out in the interaction of the elements.

Paradoxically, it was in applying the mentality of the *Bardd Newydd* to the extent that he did that Bowen produced some of his most interesting verse. The tension between everlasting truth and its representation in changing nature, for instance, is explored in 'Adgofion' (Memories, 1899). The verses wander and double back on themselves, as if the concept is emerging despite itself. The opening stanza sets the tone:

> Llygad welai Dduw ar wên mewn blodyn,
> Meinglust glywai'r Nef yn nghân aderyn,
> Meddwl fynai natur yn addoldy,
> Adgof ydyw'r cwbl erbyn heddy'. (*CBBB*, p. 151)
>
> (An eye saw the smile of God in a flower,
> A keen ear heard Heaven in birdsong,
> A mind took nature as a temple,
> All is but a memory today.)

Bowen asks the reader to consider the countryman who used 'sweet nature as a library'; Dafydd ap Gwilym, who heard the voice of his love in the song of a lark and saw her smile in the dawn; the unknown author of the *Mabinogion*, who saw Olwen's eyes in the spring and heard the rustle of her skirts in the grass of the valley. They have all perished, their visions but memories. The poet has experienced a greater change:

> Ddoe tawelwch y pentrefi gwledig,
> Heddyw gwaeddi dinas ddeffroedig;
> Ddoe alawon nant a mawl rhaiadrau,
> Heddyw blin regfeydd a thrwst cerbydau. (Ibid.)
>
> (Yesterday there was the peace of country villages,
> Today the cries of a teeming city;
> Yesterday the airs of a stream and the hymns of a waterfall,
> Today foul curses and the din of traffic.)

The mountain which God Himself created and dressed with sheep and flowers, 'a mountain which dreamed of Heaven', has been tarnished by industry. Will his own vision perish, too? The poem closes:

> Adgof heddyw ydyw canu Dafydd,
> Adgof fydd emynau'r Pêrganiedydd.
> Gwyllt yw afon amser yn myn'd heibio –
> Prin y byddaf fi a'm cân yn adgo'. (Ibid.)
>
> (Dafydd ap Gwilym's song today is a memory,
> The hymns of Pantycelyn will be the same.
> The river of time rushes wildly on –
> Scarcely will I and my song survive.)

The poem is too long, too diffuse and too unfocused to have integrity, but, curiously, Bowen's work comes closest to dignity in these semi-mystical musings, when his own search for expression is not shaped and hampered by the desire to impress a wider audience or appease adjudicators.

Oddly enough for a mystic, another voice which spoke through him was political radicalism. The Cymru Fydd (Young Wales) movement, a force for Welsh self-determination within the Liberal Party at the turn of the century, appealed. Although it failed constitutionally, it was signally more successful in its effect on popular culture. The central tenet of this radicalism, in its popular guise at least, was that Wales – through education, Nonconformism and a hazy revisionist sense of its own peasant past – was a country awaking at last to its moral mission to the world. Patriotism, disestablishment and workers' rights alike were expressions of religious zeal. Bowen was never a party animal. He lacked the patience to attend meetings or serve on committees and in all likelihood never cast a vote in an election. What inspired him was moral certitude dressed as political rhetoric.

Another insistent voice was the promptings of his contemporaries that Bowen, like Wales itself, must awaken to his purpose. Ben was a scholar and preacher dressed in the corduroy of the miner, a poet miraculously incarnate in the frail body of a young man, an heir to Wales's rural radicalism born into the industrial landscape of the Rhondda because of family circumstance. Ben Bowen became the champion of a marginalized

Wales which was desperate to prove its credentials. Their belief in him fed his belief in himself.

These competing voices can all be heard in Bowen's 'Y Deffroad Cenedlaethol' (The National Awakening), which first brought him to national attention at the age of eighteen. It is a remarkably confident piece of work, 300 lines of rhyming couplets divided into four stanzas, showing that the poet knew precisely what was expected of him. The first stanza, 'Nos' (Night), sets the scene in a series of random images as the world prepares to sleep. Even when there are flashes of metaphor, however, as in

> Mae trymder nos yn amdo ddu i'r bwthyn,
> Dystawrwydd nos yn fedd i gân aderyn . . . (Ibid., p. 1)
>
> (The heaviness of night is a black shroud over the cottage
> The silence of night a grave to the song of the bird . . .)

Bowen tends to repeat the title of the stanza, like a sedulous student exhausting the subject. By the second stanza, 'Nos a Chwsg' (Night and Sleep), night itself has become a metaphor for Wales's servitude under Catholicism. The green bay tree of true religion has been made into a crucifix to crucify again the Lord of Life. The *pryddest* then begins – in orthodox *Bardd Newydd* fashion – to employ abstract nouns and exclamation marks until, with sixteen or seventeen syllables in a line, the fabric of the whole heaves under the weight, couplets become tercets and the meaning becomes obscure:

O mor ddu, mor ddwfn ofnadwy ydyw'r nos o anwybodaeth!
Ofergoeliaeth yn cau llwybrau Gwir y Nef i'w hymwybyddiaeth;
Mae sancteiddrwydd Dydd yr Arglwydd iddi'n sathrfa llygredigaeth!
(Ibid., p. 3)

(Oh how black, how deep and awful is the night of ignorance!
Superstition closing the True paths of Heaven to its consciousness;
The sanctity of the Lord's Day has become a path of corruption!)

'Dydd a Deffro' (Day and Awakening) is a roll-call of the heroes of Cymru Fydd's historiography. It begins with Griffith Jones of Llanddowror, who taught generations to read the Bible in Welsh; Hywel Harris and Daniel Rowland, the heroes of the Methodist Revival; the incomparable hymn-writer Pantycelyn. All were eighteenth-century prophets of the awakening which would prove to be Wales's apotheosis. The couplet

> Ymdaith Nefoedd tua Chymru – dyna ydyw y Diwygiad:
> Ymdaith Cymru tua'r Nefoedd – dyna ydyw y Deffroad.
> (Ibid. p. 6)
>
> (The march of Heaven towards Wales – that is the Revival:
> The march of Wales towards Heaven – that is the Awakening.)

may be doggerel, but it epitomized the self-confidence and sense of divine destiny which underpinned late nineteenth-century radicalism. The section then lists later giants of the pulpit, praises hymnology and the institutions of Nonconformism, going on to acclaim the eisteddfod and its poets, the University of Wales and its teachers, and the novelist Daniel Owen, 'the great Raphael of Wales's life'. All have a consciousness of duty and a role to fulfil in what Bowen calls the 'harmony' of the spiritual and the democratic in the life of Wales. The final stanza, 'Breuddwyd a Byw' (Dream and Life), sets the duality of the awakening in context. The style is pure *Bardd Newydd* Platonism:

> Beth yw breuddwydio ond deffro'n cwsg-ymysgwyd?
> Calon yn tynu'i llun ei hunan yw breuddwyd:
> Breuddwyd yw Gobaith – swyn-lun Dyfodol
> O hedd yn ymdrwsio yn nrych y Presenol:
> A daw pob breuddwydio'n fwy clir – mwy hyfryd,
> Pan wedi ymgnawdoli yn ffeithiau Bywyd. (Ibid., pp. 6–7)
>
> (What is dreaming but an awakening stirring in its sleep?
> A dream is the picture the heart draws of itself:
> Hope is a dream – a mirage of a Future
> Of peace preparing itself in the mirror of the Present:

And every dream becomes clearer – more lovely,
When incarnate in the actuality of Life.)

Wales has awoken from its sleep because, like a second Arthur, its time has come. The *pryddest* closes with a final call for Wales to play its part in the 'Drama of the World', to march towards the 'Canaan of Spirituality', to be a 'Column of Holy Fire' to light the way for the nations.

More could be said, but even in a brief summary such as this two important features stand out. The first is that by the age of eighteen Ben Bowen had learned the trick of writing plausible poetry in the grand manner; second, that this plausibility consisted more in reciting the orthodoxy of Nonconformist hagiography than in expressing a personal vision. It is 'safe' verse, calculated to impress upon the adjudicators that the poet had done his homework. The names of the great and good had been learned, their potted biographies incorporated, their achievements given due attention. There was nothing unusual or untoward in the idea of a would-be poet spending time in the local library to read up on the people and events which any composition worth its salt would have to contain. Bowen was no exception. Myfyr Hefin recalls how he would take over his younger brother's work in the pit on the eve of an eisteddfod so that the necessary background reading could be done.

Bowen had to do his homework or his verse would not have been read. He worked within a tradition which demanded it. It would be wrong, however, to think of this *pryddest* as a cynical exercise in self-publicity or to regard it simply as the satisfaction of intellectual curiosity. For the young Bowen, poetry performed the function of bolstering his own belief in the orthodoxies he espoused. The very act of presenting an idea in verse became a warrant of its validity, as though the good, the beautiful and the true were inextricably linked. It was a means of self-expression with strings attached. The same can be said to some extent of all his early occasional pieces. They ooze sentimentality; but it is sentimentality with an aesthetic, a vocabulary and a purpose beyond itself. Bowen's poems are products of an acquiescent talent, guarantees of submission, to God, to his readership, to the image of the poet as a sensitive soul set apart. 'Diniweidrwydd' (Innocence) praises the beauty, the helplessness and the hidden strength of ignorance. The idea is revisited in 'Moliant Plentyn' (A Child's Praise) where the young poet declares no better music exists than the voice of a child praising his maker.

The concept of a return to innocence as a prerequisite of salvation is central to much of the early work. What has been learned must be forgotten. 'Gwneyd y Byd yn Nef' (Making the World a Heaven) begins like a child's hymn. The poet says that he is 'a friend of Jesus; his little heart is merry'; he must 'work and love' to restore the world for God:

> Anialwch drygau'r ddaear
> Yn Eden eto ddaw,
> A blodau'r nefoedd hawddgar
> Yn filoedd ar bob llaw. (Ibid., p. 17)
>
> (The desert of earth's evils
> Will become an Eden again,
> And the lovely flowers of heaven
> Will bloom in their thousands.)

The idea is expanded in the 1898 sermon, 'Y Lili' ('The Lily'), which takes its text from Matthew 6: 28–9, 'Consider the lilies of the field':

> One could hardly believe that the Sahara desert had once known the perfumes of Eden. Life today does not know Eden because Eden has no life. The world is without Eden because its life was not treated fairly. Every desert is the Eden which was once the inheritance of every life, but which was crushed by disregard and turned into a wilderness by the judgment of God . . . There would be fewer deserts in the world if the paths of Eden had never been disregarded. Eden would be seen more often if purer eyes were searching for it. And what made the world a Garden of Eden for Adam was, not so much walls around a piece of green, but because he himself was pure. The

purity of Adam, and not the beauty of the garden, made the world an Eden. The serpent in Eden would have had no sting had Adam been without sin – 'the sting of death'. (*RhBB*, pp. 137–8)

Eden is invoked again in 'Wrth yr Allor' (At the Altar), a series of *englynion* written on the occasion of a friend's wedding. Married life, he tells the young couple, will be a journey to 'Gwynfa Wen', a blessèd paradise, 'along the paths of Eden'. Bowen's elegies abound with the same prelapsarian images of flowers and gardens. The metaphor of the faded lily is sustained over ten quatrains in 'Sarah Samuel, Bryntroedgam':

> Collwyd prydferthion Eden lân,
> Collwyd aroglau'i blodau mân!
> Gwelwn yn nhrem fy lili ddrud
> Dlysni 'i swynion eto'n y byd. (*CBBB*, p. 9)

> (The beauties of fair Eden are lost,
> The scent of her tiny flowers is lost!
> We see in the gaze of my dear lily
> The loveliness of her charms still in the world.

In 'Wrth Fedd Fy Chwaer Fach' (At My Little Sister's Graveside), the poet greets his two-year-old sister as 'cenad di-ofid y Nefoedd i'r byd' ('the serene ambassador of Heaven to the world'), asserting in Wordsworthian tones that 'Rhyw freuddwyd am nefoedd yw oes plentyn bach' (The life of a tiny child is a dream of heaven.). For that reason, the pristine state of childhood should be treasured. 'Mordaith yr Ieuanc' (Youth's Voyage, 1897) is a plea for adult experience to be deferred:

> Mae'r môr o dy flaen, a gwyddost nad yw
> Ei ysgwyd aflonydd
> Ond cawell ystormydd:
> Gwell doeth nâg yw'r beiddgar mewn bâd gyda'r llyw.

> Arafa! arafa! mae'r fordaith yn faith!
> Rho drem ar y dyfnder,

Ond cadw dy hyder.
Arafa! gall brysio andwyo dy daith. (Ibid., p. 54)

(The sea lies before you, and you know that
Its wild rocking
Is a cage of storms:
The wise is better than the adventurous at the helm of the boat.

Slow down! slow down! the voyage is long!
Look at the depth,
But keep your courage.
Slow down! hurrying can ruin your journey.)

His early patriotic verse, too, makes a virtue of spiritual innocence. Faith is Wales's natural state, and doubt must be regarded as an affliction, an aberration which will pass. 'Gair o Gysur' (A Word of Comfort, 1899), for example, begins:

Paid âg ofni, Gymru,
Colli olau'r [sic] Nef;
Paid, O paid â chrynu
Wrth bob newydd lef. (Ibid., p. 141)

(Wales, be not fearful
At the loss of Heaven's light;
Do not, Oh do not tremble
At each new alarm.)

Indeed, a moment's disbelief makes the return of faith all the stronger:

Rhaid i'r storm ddiflanu –
Aros raid i'r glâs;
Cei'n felusach ganu
Wedi'r daran grâs. (Ibid.)

(The storm must disappear –
You must await fair weather;
You shall sing sweeter
After the turbulent thunder.)

'Rhaid imi Garu Cymru' (I Must Love Wales) also centres on wilful naivety:

> Rhaid imi garu Cymru –
> Sy'n fwy na'i hamheuon i gyd –
> Ga ddweyd am y Nef wrth y byd –
> Cymru gonestrwydd gweithiwr –
> Cymru unplygrwydd meddyliwr –
> Rhaid imi garu Cymru. (Ibid., p. 145)

> (I must love Wales –
> Which is greater than all her doubts –
> Which tells the world about Heaven –
> The Wales of a worker's honesty –
> The Wales of a thinker's integrity –
> I must love Wales.)

Love Wales though he did, he left it behind. His exile in South Africa was a flight from Eden, an absence forced upon him by poor health and by a growing unease with the demands which his poetry placed upon him. The rebellion began. When he wrote about Eden again, in the *pryddest* 'Gardd Eden' on his return to Wales, he was a dying man, desperate to salvage the ingenuousness which he had shunned during his time abroad.

Bowen's letters and diaries during his time in Africa offer the fullest account of his character and the development of the mythology which admirers would weave around him. He cast himself in the role of the hesitant exile, writing on board the ship which carried him to Cape Town:

> Calon ieuanc yn fy mynwes,
> Siomedigaeth yn fy hanes;
> Y mae cleddyf gwaedliw angau
> Rhwng Edenfyd Cymru a minau.
>
> Ambell ddeigryn yn fy llygad,
> Trymgwsg blin dros lawer bwriad;
> Meddwl rhoi fy oes i Gymru,
> Ond yn gorfod, gorfod cefnu. (Ibid., p. 194)

(A young heart in my breast,
Disappointment in my life;
The blood-coloured sword of death
Lies between the Eden of Wales and me.

The occasional tear in my eye,
A sad sleep over many ambitions;
Thinking to give my life to Wales,
But forced, forced to turn away.)

He had time to compose on his outward journey, with no other audience for the time being than his own sense of self. By casting himself as a reluctant voyager, he was exonerated from raising the doubts which he had hitherto suppressed. A change of tone was already apparent.

The earliest of the new verse he wrote, 'Sabbath ar y Môr' (Sabbath at Sea), was composed on 10 February. Its opening lines neatly set out the tension he felt between a desire for innocence and the pressure to acknowledge the change he was undergoing:

Erioed yn mynu credu ac erioed
Yn gorfod amheu – heddyw dyma fi
A'r wlad y sugnais gredo ar ei bron
Yn mhell, yn mhell! murmuron prudd y môr,
Fel cwynfan arall fyd, yn ymddwyshau,
Ac fel fy ysbryd inau mae y dòn,
Wrth chwilio am hedd, yn methu ar ei thaith –
Yn tori ei chalon mewn anobaith blin;
Breuddwydiais droeon y b'ai cwrdd fy Nuw
Yn sancteiddiolaf teml unigedd môr
Yn ysprydolaeth imi am fy oes:
Ond heddyw mor faterol yw fy nhrem! (Ibid., p. 196)

(Ever wishing to believe and ever
Forced to doubt – today, here I am
And the country where I learned my creed
Far, far away! the melancholy murmurs of the sea
Deepen like the lamentations of another world,
And like my spirit the waves,
Searching for peace, fail in their quest –

Break their heart in wearisome despair;
I long dreamed that to meet my God
In the sacred temple of the lonely sea
Would be an inspiration to my whole life:
But today, how material is my gaze!)

The God of his childhood was receding, he averred, chased from creation by a more knowing age:

Y mae'r Dwyfoldeb welid oesau'n ôl
Gan deidiau imi'n llanw bryn a phant,
Yn marw ar doriad dydd gwyddoniaeth fyth . . .
Mae'r byd wrth enill ffeithiau'n colli ffydd,
A ffeithiau sydd yn materoli oes. (Ibid., p. 197)

(The Divinity which my forefathers saw
Filling hill and dale in ages past,
Dies constantly at the dawn of science . . .
The world loses faith as it gains facts,
And facts make the age material.)

Piece by piece, Bowen would spend the last two years of his life painfully unpicking his own faith and reconstructing it. His early days in South Africa were full of hasty conclusions. A consciousness of his own fame had followed him. *Y Darian*, a south Wales weekly, had made a request for regular bulletins from him, as had O. M. Edwards in his capacity as editor of *Cymru'r Plant*, a recently launched children's magazine in the style of his more established *Cymru*. Although Bowen affected to resent the intrusion, writing to Myfyr Hefin in March 1901 to ask, 'Why must a young boy have his name constantly before the public?' (*BBNA*, p. 11), the fear that his popularity would fade in his absence from Wales made him uneasy. 'Beware of praise!' he wrote in an English letter to an old schoolfriend,

for it favours conceit, and that means the death of everything noble in you. But when you have a kind word to tell me, do so, freely, and I will thank you *'o ddyfnder enaid'* [from the depth of my soul] for it. Praise is to every-day life like butter to bread. (Ibid., pp. 9–10)

He was aware, too, that the public contributions which had paid his passage placed obligations upon him: 'Wales', he commented to Myfyr Hefin, 'has bought me' (Ibid., p. 13). Ironically, it strengthened the desire to remain in Africa: he sent for information on university courses in Cape Town and toyed with the idea of staying there to work as a missionary.

The desire to compete had not diminished. Within days of his arrival, on 26 February 1901, he was beginning to map out the plan for 'Y Diwygiwr' (The Reformer), an *awdl* for that year's National Eisteddfod in Merthyr, enclosing sample *englynion* for his brother's comments. By 26 March the work was complete. 'No doubt I can be beaten,' he remarked, 'but not easily, and in conception I believe that I shall be among the masterpieces of the competition' (Ibid., p. 12). The completed work was sent to Myfyr Hefin on Easter Monday, 1 April. It had a tendency in places to be too deep to be acceptable, he conceded, but that was a good failing in 'a superficial age'.

In the same letter he announced that his health was slowly improving, despite bouts of dysentery during his first fortnight, with pains 'which bent me double like a folded book'. His brother's requests for him to rest were ignored:

> I would like a life of complete rest for some years, but you know that rest in the sense of not working does not belong to us as a family. As soon as I can stand, I insist on walking. When I can walk, I insist on running. Having learned to run, a desire to fly. When flying, to burn my wings in the bonfires of suns until I find myself again on my face in the mud of the world. Remember that saying this isn't poetry but plain speaking. Oh, that my mind could rest in all the events of life and be one with their music. It finds its chief joy in setting itself to work . . . As I ponder my future, remember that I am like Noah changing his surroundings, releasing my dove across the pathless face of the flood. (Ibid., pp. 12–13)

The explanation, with its allusion to Daedalus and Icarus, suggests strongly that by 1901 Bowen's ambitions were driven as much by a fear of failure as by any desire to succeed. The image has a recklessness about it. The fall face down in the mud of the world was inevitable; only bravado and constant activity could postpone it.

The humid climate of Cape Town did not agree with him, and the town had recently suffered an outbreak of jaundice. By the end of April he had taken up an invitation to move to the drier ground of Kimberley, more than 3,000 ft above sea level. Due to the Boer War, travel was by permit only, and the delay infuriated him. When he reached Kimberley after a 36-hour train journey, the effect on his health was immediate: 'I do not believe that I have ever breathed more splendid air. My lungs unconsciously opened to welcome it' (Ibid., p. 19), he wrote to his brother within a day of his arrival. His enthusiasm, however, did not last long. A restlessness overtook him. On 18 May he would write of Kimberley, and South Africa more generally:

> It is a country which has failed to develop a mental life. There are strange ideas in the locals' heads. Dance is everything and bending a knee nothing, and I utterly fail to see that a man who knows about nothing other than the twists and turns of commerce has a broader intellect than the man who knows only his Bible and his hymn book. The chief danger for Africa is money. Everyone from the greatest to the least sets his sights on making money . . . More respect is paid to an ass in Wales than to a missionary in Africa. (Ibid., p. 22)

He had travelled halfway around the world, only to find himself back in the Treorci of his childhood.

As early as 1897 Bowen had shown a talent in his sermons for hinting at unorthodoxy. South Africa would finally crush any residual desire he had to preach and push him eventually into what was heresy in the eyes of his sponsors back in Moriah. Away from the constrictions of regular organized worship Bowen drifted into overt pantheism, referring to God as 'The Immortal' or 'the great immortal mind of the world', arguing that a divine spark existed in all living things, seeing himself as a prophet. He anticipated the criticism which would come, asking his brother not to love him for his orthodoxy, 'lest perhaps a day will come when you will slander me for it': 'Rather, love your brother because you cannot fail to. Strengthen your love, if you insist with his success, but, chiefly, with his seriousness. A wave of unpopularity is breaking; be with me in that terrible day' (Ibid., p. 31). He enclosed with the letter a snatch of verse, written on his outward journey, which hinted at his state of mind:

> Beth yw Duw
> Ond enw ar amherffeithrwydd deall dyn?
> Ond enw prydferth ar ddirgelwch blin?
> Gwyn yw y bryn o bell, gwyn, gwyn gan wawr,
> Ond wedi cyrraedd dim ond llwydni hwyr
> A'r wawr a'm galwai ymlaen yn suddo i'r nos!
> A minnau'n wylo'n ofer ar ei bedd,
> Ac fel y nos ar flaen y wawr, mae Duw
> Yn codi ei babell ar ddynesiad dyn,
> Yn codi ei babell ac yn mynd, yn mynd! (Ibid.)

> (What is God
> But a name for the imperfection of man's understanding?
> But a beautiful name for a tiresome mystery?
> The hill from afar appears white, white, white with dawn,
> But when I reach it there is only the greyness of evening
> And the dawn which called me on has sunk into night!
> And I weep vainly on its grave,
> While God, like the night before the dawn,
> Removes his tent at the approach of man,
> Removes his tent and is gone, is gone!)

When one compares the tone of this piece with Bowen's early devotional work, the contrast is stark. 'Carwn Fod' (I Would Love to Be), for example, where the poet asks to be 'in God / Like a star in heaven', and the hymns 'Y Boreuddydd Hyfryd Draw' (The Lovely Morning Yonder) and 'Pwyso ar Iesu' (Leaning on Jesus), have a lyricism grounded in certainty. What tension there is, is manufactured. The poet frightens himself into doubting God the better to savour the reassurance of his presence. Here, though, the images and the resonances are darker, the uncertainty more thorough. God has fled, and flees constantly, before his creation. There is a hint of more, too, than an assertion that man searches vainly for God. The quotation above ends with two rhetorical lines which tease with their ambiguity:

> Ai Duw yn darfod yn natblygiad dyn
> Yw ystyr Duw yn marw dros y byd? (Ibid.)

A literal translation would be: 'Is the meaning of God's death for the world / The death of God in the development of man?' The meaning is still obscure. What Bowen is attempting to ask, one suspects, is whether God's death for the world (at the Crucifixion) implies that God has died, too, in the history of man; that the Crucifixion means the ending of a direct relationship between man and God. An event seen through the eyes of orthodoxy as the fulfilment of a covenant is seen here as the breaking of that covenant.

The question of the divinity of Christ preoccupied him. In a letter to Myfyr Hefin on 3 August 1901 he wrote:

> I prefer to say that He is the most divine [human] whom the world ever saw, or, in other words, that humanity is seen in its true quality in Him, i.e. divinity – the rose of humanity in full bloom . . . Has anyone ever been able to draw a line between man and God? No. What God is, I am. If you insist on saying that Jesus is God, very well. I too say that, and I worship. If you say that there is something in the nature of Jesus which is not in my nature, or that there is a 'gulf' between Him and me – stay your hand and stand back! After you have thought as much about the subject as I have, i.e., after you have thought until you cannot sleep at night, yearned for the light until you see your constitution fall apart, you will have room to talk, and not before. (Ibid., p. 38)

The idea that mental suffering should be viewed as a warrant of truth is revealing. It would not be fanciful to suggest that Bowen underwent what amounted to a breakdown in South Africa. In his letters home, intellectual and spiritual self-regard jostle against loathing: for the intellectual poverty of South Africa; for the tenets of Baptist faith which he had chosen to embrace as a youth; for the academic world he simultaneously dismissed and so much wished to be a part of; for the eisteddfod clique which he believed had conspired against him to deprive him of the recognition he deserved; for his own failing body. His poetry becomes for him both therapy and a code of dissent. He speaks of his fear of betraying his unorthodoxy in 'Y Diwygiwr' and asks that the poem be 'buried respectfully until the day of its resurrection' (Ibid.). 'Y Diwygiwr' will be discussed in more detail later in this chapter. For the moment it is enough to note that, for Myfyr Hefin, his younger brother's increasing disenchantment with conventional Nonconformism was a cause for alarm. In the foreword to *Ben Bowen yn Neheudir Affrica*, he goes to some lengths to emphasize that Bowen remained a true Christian and died in a state of grace. His doubts, he averred, perished with him.

In the mean time, the question of how to spend his time profitably bothered him. Freed from financial concerns, but still mindful of his health, Bowen found that a restive spirit and a wealth of possibilities were a debilitating combination. He confessed to his sister, Ann, in May 1901 that he felt a tension between the desire to see 'the unity which lies beneath all forms of life and belief and the one thing which demands a life of devotion': 'And a man must do something, but he cannot, by his nature, do everything. It is possible to do something for everything, or everything for something, but a man cannot do everything for everything without first being God' (Ibid., p. 24).

On medical advice, an early return to Wales was out of the question. Haemorrhages – 'the red light', as he called them – were still common. By mid-May he had accepted an invitation to Simla in India. He later decided against it. Other schemes for periods in Egypt and Australia would follow. Altogether, Bowen intended to stay away for two full years before facing what he

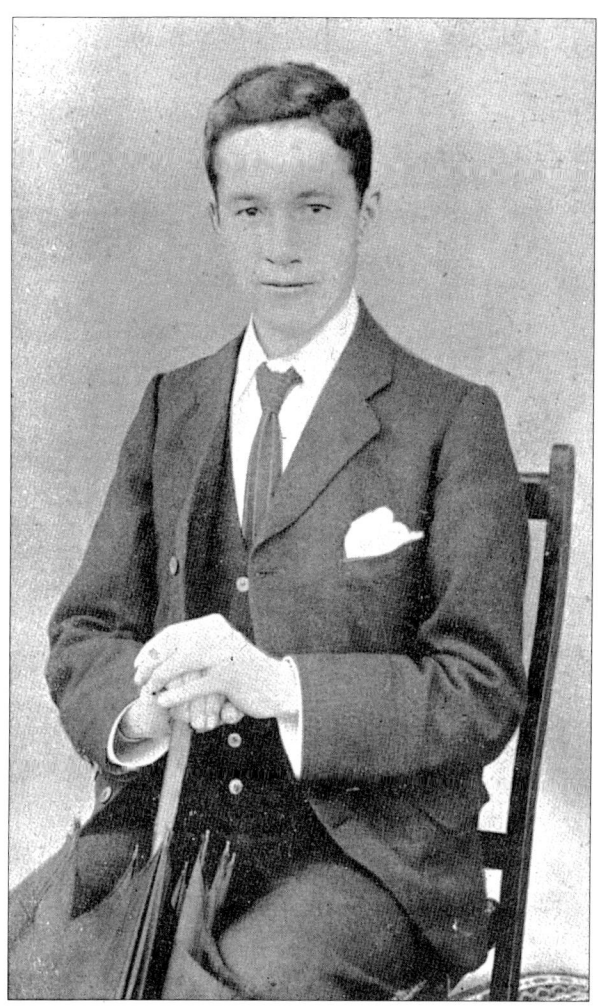

Ben Bowen in Kimberley, 1901.

called 'the Canaan of Wales. If God has another plan – all's well!' (Ibid., p. 23).

By June Bowen had found work as a clerk with the Army Service Corps, earning 10s. a day and food. It broke the monotony, but news that two former clerks had had to leave because of TB forced him to leave after only a month. By 20 July, Bowen realized that he had not won with 'Y Diwygiwr' at Merthyr – 'more of a surprise than a disappointment', he told his brother. The *awdl* had been composed, he argued, 'not for the Chair but for the peace of my mind' (Ibid., p. 134). The surprise seems more than the product of wounded self-belief; there is an element of twisted self-perception here which goes beyond presumption. There is a genuine inability on Bowen's part to see why a poem into which he had put so much of himself had failed to impress the adjudicators.

A year before, one might have expected a dissertation on the fathers of the Methodist Revival, a revamp, perhaps, of lines from his highly orthodox 'Williams Pantycelyn' (1900), coupled with high-flown praises for Hywel Harris and the rest. Indeed, the original composition contained a canto entitled 'Offrwm Cymru' (The Offering of Wales) listing the great and the good in Wales's Nonconformist past. The entire canto was subsequently excised. By 1901 the direction he wished to take was quite different. It would be glib to say that 'Y Diwygiwr' is autobiographical. A more profitable approach would be to say that it can be usefully read as a commentary on Bowen's state of mind as South Africa became more familiar, or at least less alien, to him.

Was Bowen unconsciously influenced by the location of that year's National Eisteddfod in Merthyr? The *awdl* could be entitled 'Y Merthyr' (The Martyr) without detriment. In the 'Outline' which precedes the ode proper, Ben Bowen argues that a revival presupposes the existence of 'a world gone wrong'. The poem thereafter is predicated on the idea of a paradoxical creation where pain and death become the objects of true art, where the Reformer sets right what nature herself cannot heal and suffers the consequence. The Reformer is a guarantee of God's care for His creation and at the same time a sacrifice to that care. He gives of himself so that God's will might be made manifest. The work opens with a series of *englynion* in praise of nature's beauty, with clear overtones of *Bardd Newydd* divine–material correspondence. By the second canto, the mood has changed:

> O mae ingoedd – mae angau – a rhaib oer
>   Y bedd – yn myd blodau!
> Ac o fedydd gofidiau – rhed o'r ddôl,
>   Fôr marwnadol furmur eu nodau.
>
> Er ei hoen, mae drwy anian – boenau byw
>   Yn ben ar y cyfan;
> Cedwir yn mysg adar mân lawer pryd
>   Si am aeth adfyd nes methu 'hedfan.
>
> Mae dan fy mywyd inau – ddiwaelod
>   Ddiluw o ofidiau;
> Enbyd wyneb ei dònau – a'm dychryn,
>   A mynaf ofyn am Nef a'i Hafau . . .
>
> A mi fy hun ymofynaf – beth – beth
>   Yw y byd a garaf?
> Onid yw pob canaid Haf
>   Yn gwywo ar fron gauaf? (CBBB, p. 173)

> (O there are agonies – is death – and the cold greed
>   Of the grave – in the world of flowers!
> And from the baptism of cares – there runs from the meadow,
>   The deathly sea of the murmur of their notes.
>
> For all its vigour, there is throughout nature – the pains of life
>   Crowning all;
> Among the tiny birds – many times
>   There is a whisper of awful affliction which prevents their flight.
>
> There is in my own life – a bottomless
>   Flood of woes;
> The dreadful surface of its waves – frightens me,
>   And I must ask for Heaven and its Summers . . .

And I ask myself – what – what
　Is the world I love?
　Does not every blessèd Summer
　Wilt on the breast of Winter?)

Bowen's dystopia, his 'world gone wrong', is delineated in a nightmare chain of *englynion* reminiscent of Gerard Manley Hopkins's late sonnets and shot through with the very twentieth-century idea of a God fled from His creation every bit as affecting as the early work of T. Gwynn Jones:

'Ddaw Haf i ran amddifaid – ac addfwyn
　Guddfa i wallgofiaid?
　Ac i anian ein gweiniaid
　Onid yw byw'n boen di-baid? . . .

Onid nofio dan nifwl – amheuaeth
　O hyd mae y meddwl
　A fyna chwilio'n fanwl
　Am hardd wir mewn byd mor ddwl? (Ibid., p. 174)

(Shall Summer come to aid orphans – and be a sweet
　Refuge for lunatics?
　For those who are weaklings
　Is not life an unending agony? . . .

Is not the mind which seeks – dutifully
　To find true beauty
　In such a senseless world as this
　Always swimming in a mist of doubt?)

The *englynion* work because in them Bowen has consciously set aside the self-taught lessons of five years before. There is nothing epigrammatic or fixed here, nothing mannered, nothing 'safe'. The canto is marred by arch couplets such as

Onid yfed y dafarn
Dröa fyd i adwy'r Farn? (Ibid., p. 175)

(Does not drinking in the tavern
Lay the world open to Judgement?)

but the overall effect is of controlled despair. Even nature, for Bowen a mirror held up to the infinite, is powerless to save herself:

> Ha! Natur deg! hwnt troed hi! – nid o gaeth
> Oror naturiaeth mae'r wawr yn tori.
>
> Ar ingoedd nac ar angau – ni fedda
>   Foddion i greu golau;
> Chwerwder ddwg carchardŷ'r ddau – i fy rhan;
> Ac ni all anian mwy gynull hoenau. (Ibid.)
>
> (Ah, fair Nature! let her be turned away – the dawn
>   will not break
> On the horizon of things natural.
>
> She possesses no way – of shedding light
>   On agonies or on death;
> The prison of both brings me bitterness;
> And nature can no longer cheer me.)

By the beginning of the third canto, Bowen has painted himself into a metaphysical corner. His way of extricating himself is ingenious but flawed. There is redemption only in suffering, he asserts, in the denial of beauty:

> Sut daw hanes daioni – yn amlwg
>   Ond drwy deimlo bryntni?
> Daw y wlad deimla dlodi – eto'n llon;
> Ei hing a'i chwynion yw angau'i chyni. (Ibid., p. 176)
>
> (How can the history of goodness – become clear
>   But through feeling cruelty?
> The land that experiences poverty – will be cheerful
>   again;
> Its agony and complaint mean the death of its
>   hardship.)

What follows is a series of *englynion* in which the idea merely appears to be reiterated. 'Complaints are the condition of progress', Bowen declares; 'God gives daybreak to an uneasy soul' (Ibid., p. 177). On the face of it, the idea is straightforward enough. It hinges on a succession of oppositions between suffering and salvation, the inherent distress of earthly life set against heavenly bliss, an acceptance of the paradox of a just God in an unjust world, the need for discomfort the better to appreciate divine justice. Here and there, however, a more perverse assertion is made:

> Heb waeau ni fa'i [sic] bywyd – yn y byd;
>   Croes yw balm pob adfyd;
>   Caf wynfa y cyfanfyd
>   Yn nhrist wae y Crist o hyd. (Ibid.)
>
> (Without its woes there would be no life – in the world;
>   A cross is the balm for all torment;
>   I find the rapture of the whole world
>   Continually in Christ's distress.)

It is here, in all likelihood, that Bowen's misgivings about the unacceptability of 'Y Diwygiwr' lie. The opposition established earlier in the poem between suffering and joy is reworked and reshaped to such an extent that another less wholesome idea emerges. Rather than gratitude for Christ's redemptive sacrifice, the poet comes close to revelling in it. In imitating Christ, the Reformer is cast in the role of masochist:

> Gwae yr oes ydyw ei gryd, – a'i loes hi
>   Deifl swyn i'w ieuenctyd;
>   E' fyn feiau yn fywyd,
>   A Duw yn ddelfryd o hyd. (Ibid.)
>
> (The woe of the age is his cradle – and its agony
>   Gives charm to his youth:
>   He makes wrongs the stuff of life,
>   And God a constant ideal.)

Not only that, as the concept runs away with him, Bowen places the Reformer at one with Christ in Gethsemane and on the Cross. By the end of the canto he has become a second Deliverer, indistinguishable from the Son of God as judge and saviour:

> Onid pwynt ei enaid pur
> Ar fyw oes ddyry fesur?
> Efe yw collfarn ei fyd,
> A thwf ei obaith hefyd. (Ibid., p. 179)
>
> (Does not his pure soul
> Measure the living age?
> He is the condemnation of his world,
> And the growth of its hope also.)

He is of 'the unpolluted bloodline of the Lord Himself', Bowen announces. He performs the function of redeemer:

> Ac onid yn ei gyni
> Ef daw'r oes at fywyd Rhi? (Ibid., p. 180)
>
> (And through his adversity
> Does not the age come to the life of the Lord?)

These are treacherous theological waters, hardly the subject for an untrained critic to explore. But it is evident that Bowen's image of the expiatory suffering of the Reformer calls into question his view of the Atonement, the uniqueness of the Passion and – by extension – the very divinity of Christ. What can be said with certainty is that a young man far from home, emboldened by intellectual presumption and weighed down by doubt, went further than he could have foreseen in fashioning a theology around a subject which the eisteddfod committee at Merthyr must have set with no regard as to its potential for controversy. It is ironic that the *awdl* ends with the *englyn* which Myfyr Hefin claimed to have heard his brother repeat countless times as he lay dying and which, as executor and editor, he later took as evidence of Bowen's reconciliation to conventional Christianity:

> Ymdawelaf, mae dwylo – Duw ei Hun
>   Danaf yn mhob cyffro;
> Yn nwfn swyn ei fynwes O
> Caf lonydd – caf le i huno. (Ibid., p. 189)
>
> (I shall be still, the hands – of God Himself
>   Are beneath me in every commotion;
> In the deep charm of His breast
> I shall have peace – have a place to sleep.)

How does 'Y Diwygiwr' rate as poetry? Flabby, repetitive and, as has been suggested, intellectually confused, it is nevertheless a key text in understanding Bowen's ambition to produce an aesthetic capable of marrying his self-appointed roles of poet and prophet. In a letter to a family friend, written on the same day that he confided in Myfyr Hefin his disbelief at the decision not to chair him in Merthyr, Bowen wrote:

> What is a moth compared with a man? Surely, it is more than man is in comparison with God. Still, let us not despair because we are such insignificant beings, but remember that, although God is incomparably greater than we, He is no other than we. We partly are what He completely is. God is naught else than an Infinity of love, of intelligence, of music and of beauty, and all these are ours – are they not? Are we not capable of being captivated by beauty, lost in music and entranced in love? (*BBNA*, p. 35)

In true *Bardd Newydd* fashion, Bowen had always cast himself in the role of interpreter of things divine, a conduit through which the unseen might become visible to others. His early poetry might usefully be compared to iconography: disinterested, conformist and controlled. As his faith in conventional Christianity receded during his stay in South Africa, the emphasis shifted from product to producer. Poetry became for him a personal means of uniting with God, its creation an infinitesimal hint at the divine exercise of love, intelligence and music. On 10 August he wrote to Myfyr Hefin: 'I do not write for critics, but in submission to a higher life which makes my human nature divine' (Ibid.,

p. 42). With 'Y Diwygiwr', the process began of allowing his sense of himself as a poet to dictate his theology. Writing in exile, no longer a member of any church and reading widely but with no system or tutor, he fell in love with the creations of his own imagination. His poetry and the ideas it generated became a barrier between him and the awareness of his physical decay. In the 3 August letter to Myfyr Hefin already cited, he wrote: 'In the catacombs of dead creeds there was a danger that tuberculosis could come in. I am now too elevated in an atmosphere of divinity for the seeds of tuberculosis to disturb me' (Ibid., p. 39). He dismissed his brother's concerns:

> Do not worry about me! I know that you cannot look at things in the same light as me, and understand that God does not wish you to. Carry on along the same paths as mother and father. Do not believe that I am not with you, and do not believe that I have lost the way. I have not. The only difference is this: you look about you in leisurely fashion at green fields and gardens of flowers. I look forward to the storm of nineteenth-century doubt disappearing on the horizon, and the great day of the future breaking over the face of God. (Ibid.)

By August 1901, then, Bowen could convince himself that his faith was secure. The young man who six months previously had written of his fear that God was retreating before the material progress of man, celebrated his new-found faith in 'Goleuni y Byd' (The Light of the World), written in one furious week and dated 19 September. The best way to deal with science, he had evidently decided, was to abstract it out of existence:

> Ar ol materoldeb hir,
>   Mae y cread eto'n fyw!
> Ac wedi cwestiynau gau y gwir,
>   Codi mae'r byd
>   Yn wridog ei rudd,
>   Ac yn ieuanc ei fryd,
>   O'r diwedd i'r dydd
> Sydd yn torri ar feibion Duw! (*CBBB*, p. 197)

> (After an age of materialism
>   Creation lives again!
> And after false questions in search of truth,
>   The world rises
>   With blushing cheek,
>   And youthful countenance,
>   At last into the day
> That breaks for the sons of God!)

The woes of the world which had preoccupied him in 'Y Diwygiwr' are dismissed with a gesture of wilful ignorance:

> Ystryw ariangar fryd,
> Fradwriaeth a rhyfel erch,
> Fallder godineb yr oes,
> A mam a'i dwylo yn waed!
> Diolch – 'wyr neb ond Duw
> Ddyfnder trueni dyn –
> I lawr y bo'r llen! (Ibid., p. 189)

> (Deceitful, money-loving desire,
> Treachery and dreadful war,
> The corruption of the age's adultery,
> And a mother with bloody hands!
> Thanks – nobody but God
> Knows the depth of man's misery –
> Let the curtain fall!)

Bowen left the fate of the world in the hands of God – the Immortal Mind. 'Cyffes Awen' (The Muse's Confession), 'Plyg ar Blyg o Niwl ar Daen' (Fold Upon Fold of Spreading Mist) and 'One God', written around the same time, reiterated the same cosmic unconcern. 'Cyfrinach' (A Secret) entreated the reader:

> Paid â chwyno
>   Ar dy ran:
> Y mae osgo
>   Duw 'mhob man.

> Côd dy lygad
> At y dydd:
> Myn o'r cread
> Orsedd ffydd. (Ibid., p. 210)
>
> (Do not complain
> At your state:
> The presence of God
> Is everywhere.
>
> Raise your eye
> Up to the day:
> Make of creation
> A throne of faith.)

Bowen had settled the argument to his own satisfaction by accommodating mysticism and materialism. As in so many other respects – in a patriotism which could argue for Welsh self-determination and praise the exploits of Cecil Rhodes, homesickness for the Rhondda coupled with a desire never to live there again, an attraction to and fear of the pulpit – he revelled in paradox. He was, he confessed to Myfyr Hefin, 'an unbeliever who believes and adores more than the majority of the religious men of Wales . . . I am working out my own salvation' (*BBNA*, p. 51). The scientific progress of man, moreover, was now 'a journey towards eternal peace and work'. He recommended the study of science to his brother as an essential adjunct and counterbalance to his theology: 'The intellectual progress of the world is in the hands of Science, and the Scientist is the Moses of the Present and the Future' (Ibid.). He even felt moved to compose a song in praise of the microbe.

'Goleuni y Byd' won Bowen the chair at the London Eisteddfod in February 1902. It was to be his last public recognition. More signficantly, in composing it he had reached a compromise with God which he found spiritually uplifting and intellectually satisfying and which, crucially, excused him at last from the career as a preacher which others had predicted for him. On 10 August he confided to Myfyrfab, a cousin living in Felinfoel, Llanelli:

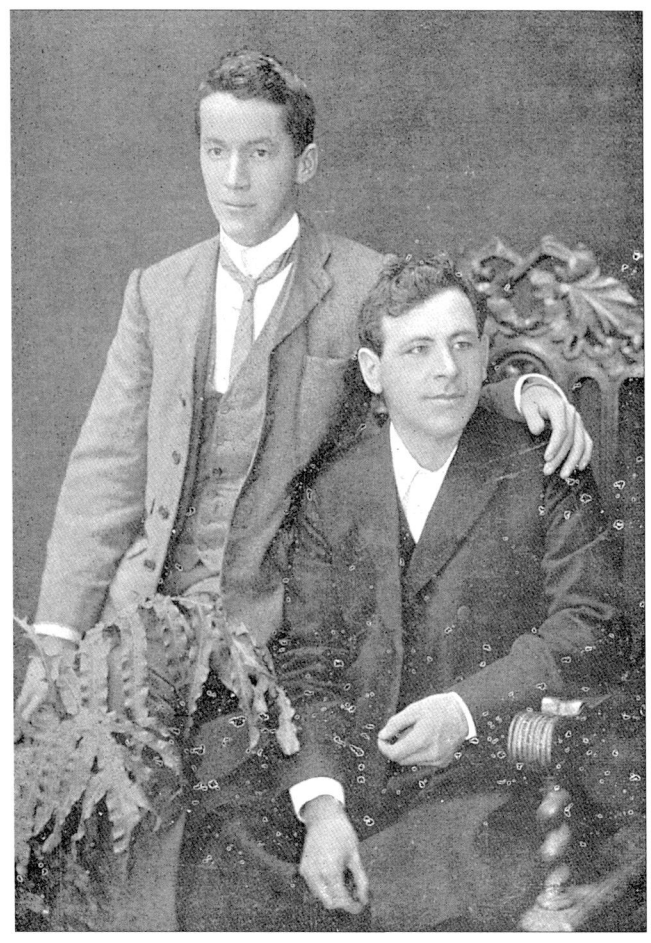

Ben Bowen (left) with Dyfnallt at the National Eisteddfod in Bangor, 1902.

I suppose . . . that my denomination will be disappointed that I am turning my back on the Pulpit, if I read the signs of the times aright. I do not have the constitution for such work, and indeed, my mind has failed completely to give life to dogma although I have made an honest effort in God's name through four years of Hell. By now I worship God on the altar of the mountain, in the scent of flowers in the holy place of the sunshine and in the temple of the blue sky. The kingdom of heaven is literally alive for me. (Ibid., p. 42)

It was to be a short-lived relief.

Chapter III

THE SECOND HALF OF 1901 WAS FILLED WITH A TENSE ENERGY. BOWEN began daily lessons in German, followed the course of the Boer War as it broke around him and planned with a friend to run a market garden on the outskirts of town. In all the busyness, the poor reception given to 'Y Diwygiwr' in Merthyr, which had momentarily caused him to doubt whether he would compete in an eisteddfod again and enter into a pointless debate with one of the adjudicators, was forgotten. By the end of August he had written 300 lines of 'Ymadawiad Arthur' (The Passing of Arthur), the subject for the chair in Bangor in 1902. The *awdl* was complete by 5 October. In its composition, he reverted to the method he had employed as an ambitious young miner in Treorci. His letters home make repeated requests for books on the Arthurian Cycle from Malory to Tennyson. Myfyr Hefin was pressed into service to read and transcribe the entries on Arthur, Mordred, Merlin, Guinevere, Bedivere and the rest from the Welsh encyclopaedia, *Y Gwyddoniadur*, and to comb through Geoffrey of Monmouth and Giraldus Cambrensis. Bowen's broader vision, however, was less piecemeal than the bibliography might suggest. The topic appealed to him and he sought to make it his own:

> 'Arthur' suits me perfectly, – a man who turns his back on his country, whose past has been a failure, and who crosses the sea to a wonderful and healthy country to recover, with an uncertain and doubtful intention of returning to fight again to make the nation a kingdom of purity and one with the world at large. Ben Bowen is Bangor's 'Arthur'. Whether Ben Bowen will win the chair I know not, and it does not matter to me. My only aim is to compose a beautiful piece of work as an embodiment of truth. (*BBNA*, p. 72)

Readers familiar with the history of twentieth-century Welsh literature will savour the irony. Bowen's 'Ymadawiad Arthur', whatever its merits, can only ever be viewed with parted eye. The *awdl* competition at the Bangor Eisteddfod of 1902, as has been mentioned, marked the public recognition of a man seven years Bowen's senior: Thomas Gwynn Jones. His winning composition charmed the adjudicators, redefined the literary aesthetic for a generation and became an instant classic. Bowen could not compete. Bangor aged him overnight. It made him forever the loser, forever the last, lost hope of Victorian literature. By the time it had been composed and sent, its author had already decided to return to Wales, his health fundamentally no better.

Bowen's 'Ymadawiad' must be read, therefore, not only in the unflattering light of Gwynn Jones's success, but also as a counterpoint to the confidence of his own poems in late 1899, as the *Southampton* carried him to Cape Town. What the *awdl* omits is as striking as what it contains. There is no narrative thread; rather, the story is told and retold in a series of set-piece monologues centring on the twin themes of betrayal and redemption. The overall impression is anti-climactic – or, more accurately, post-climactic. Bowen's Arthur almost dies a broken cynic:

> O ymado siomedig! – gwron Duw
>   Geir yn deyrn gwywedig:
>   Wele mae fel noethlwm wig,
>   Yn fynwent Gauaf unig! . . .
>
> Sancteiddrwydd yn aflwyddiant; – a chariad
>   Yn chwerwedd; gogoniant
>   Yn chwareubeth i fethiant;
>   A gwae dros obeithion gant. (*CBBB*, p. 217)
>
> (Oh disappointed departure! – God's champion
>   Is a shrunken leader;
>   See, he is like a bare wood
>   A graveyard of lonely winter! . . .

> Holiness defeated: – and love
> > Become bitter; glory
> > The plaything of failure;
> > And a hundred intentions dashed.)

However, the poet intervenes to rescue him with *Bardd Newydd* sophistry:

> Ond mae rhywbeth mewn methiant – yn arwain
> > I burach gogoniant;
> > A cheir yn fy ymdrech I
> > Allweddi gloewach llwyddiant . . .
>
> Fel y myno'r Iôr o hyd!
> Oesau gyda'u gwaeau'i gyd
> Yn ei drem yn flodau dry,
> Yn ei salm yn nodau sy. (Ibid., pp. 220–1)
>
> (But there is something in failure – which leads
> > To a purer glory;
> > And there are in my struggle
> > The keys of a brighter success . . .
>
> Let it be always as God wills!
> Ages with all their woes
> Turn to flowers in his sight,
> To notes in his heavenly psalm.)

The *awdl* then becomes one general exodus. Guinevere is absolved (as much for her beauty as any moral virtue, it appears) and spirited away to her own private Avalon; Bedivere dies acquiescent and grateful; Merlin is portrayed as a prophet, 'whispering the intentions of the Lord'. And Avalon itself, an extension of Merlin's presence, although described with a sensuousness which echoes Gwynn Jones's own command of *cynghanedd*, is recast in distinctive Ben Bowen fashion:

> Mae palas o heuldes ym mynwes y môr;
> A'r wawrddydd mor ddedwydd yn gwylio ei ddôr;

A'i barlwr o berlau
O dan y beilch dònau
Yn gartref dirgelion sy'n weision yr Iôr.

Gwê o enfysau ar dònau y dydd;
A'r nos, yn fy nyfnder, y lloer a'r ser sydd
Yn fil dros fy nhawel borfeydd;
Diderfyn ysplander wna amser yn un
Ei wawl a haul y tragwyddol ei hun
Erioed fu fy nghyfrin rodfeydd. (Ibid., p. 228)

(There is a palace of sunshine in the bosom of the ocean;
And the dawn watches its portals with joy;
And its parlour of pearls
Beneath the proud waves
Are a home for the mysteries of the servants of God.

A web of rainbows light the waves by day;
And by night, in my depths, the sun and stars
Shine in thousands across my peaceful meadows;
An endless splendour makes its light the same
As the eternal sun itself
Ever in my mystic ways.)

Bowen never came closer to embracing romanticism, but at the same time was never further from it. The language is lavish, the images are rich; but the sensibility which informs them is pure *Bardd Newydd*. His Avalon is an Eden: a place where guilt is forgotten and innocence restored, 'a sacred bosom of youth', as the final line describes it.

By the time of the Eisteddfod itself that September, Bowen had found himself unexpectedly back in Wales. His final few months in Africa were touched as always by controversy. First, there was his defence of concentration camps for Boer prisoners. 'Nobody in Kimberley', he assured readers of the *South Wales News* on 10 December 1901, 'has better air to breathe, finer sunshine to bask in than the Boer refugees. So far as the comforts of life are concerned, the vast majority of these people are better off than they ever were.' Sympathy was absurd: 'It is no empty dream of a poet, no theory of a blind philosopher, but a glaring fact of history that ignorant and filthy nations helpless in their degradation must be trampled to dust in the eternal march of mind.' The article, followed by one in a similar vein in the *Western Mail* in February 1902, provoked the type of reaction which always seemed to thrill him in the two papers' largely pro-Boer readership. 'Perhaps', he confided in his brother, 'God has placed his finger on my breast and pointed out the weak spot in time for me to see that the Press is my pulpit after all' (*BBNA*, p. 192). By the beginning of 1902 his letters home had taken on a distinctly political tone, their contents the drafts of pieces he toyed with writing for a wider audience. The desire to see his name in print stayed with him until his death: his letters home would often ask that a half-dozen or more copies of his published material be sent out to Africa for distribution among friends and acquaintances.

It could be argued that Bowen was never happier than in the early months of 1902: his health continued to improve; 'Goleuni y Byd' was chaired at the eisteddfod in Exeter Hall, London, which augured well for 'Ymadawiad Arthur'; he had leisure to read and think; the ties between him and Wales could be maintained on his own terms; he cherished dreams of a quiet return, living as a country postman, writing at his leisure. But the same love of contentiousness, the same naive desire for self-publicity which fuelled his poetry and his politics, rushed in to fill the void. A piece, 'Bedyddiwr at Fedyddwyr' (A Baptist to Baptists) was sent to *Y Geninen* between Christmas and New Year. The reaction to it finally drove him out of his denomination.

'Bedyddiwr at Fedyddwyr' is written in the unmistakable Bowen style. It is passionate, self-important and rather dull: the sort of thing young theological students fancy themselves writing. For a man touched by intimations of the infinite, he dwells prosaically on the biblical ordinance, or lack of it, for adult baptism. He displays his awareness of fashionable criticism by referring to the historical reliability of the various gospels and peppers his text with rhetorical questions.

It was a quixotic attempt to undermine the foundations of the denomination. Bowen sought to portray it as an act of moral obligation, although one can guess at the secondary response he hoped to provoke from his admission that he half-intended it as the first in a series comprising 'A Preacher to Preachers', 'A Poet to Poets', 'A Nonconformist to Nonconformists' and 'A Welshman to Welshmen'. His intention as preacher, Nonconformist, poet and Welshman was to define himself in opposition to others; to be as much contrary as controversial. In the event, there was no series. It hardly seemed necessary. As an exercise in dissent, 'Bedyddiwr at Fedyddwyr' on its own did what Bowen both feared and longed for. Friends who had begged him not to write were outraged; Moriah, which had sponsored his stay in South Africa, disowned him; the Baptist weekly *Seren Cymru* carried a letter calling him 'a soft-headed and base-minded youth' (*CBBB*, p. lxvi). There was method in the soft-headedness. Bowen returned to Wales a free man: he owed nothing and was not obliged to anyone. He had committed social suicide. His words to his brother as he set off to Wales in the wake of the article said it all:

> Breadth of mind, depth of spirit, an unyielding faith in the 'Great I Am', and let petty creeds go where they will! Let the praise of man cease too! Heaven preserve me from writing anything for praise, and lead me ever to all truth! I do not give a rotten potato for the opinion of theological quacks, as you well know. And perhaps my disdain for these quacks is as great as my respect for the God whom they seek to place in a halfpenny balance. (Ibid.)

Perhaps, indeed.

He sailed from Port Elizabeth on 27 May 1902, arriving in London in mid-July. Queen Victoria was dead and the coronation of Edward VII was imminent. His outward journey cost him £24; the return was a third of the price, a slow, exhausting journey along the eastern route to Aden and across the Red Sea before travelling overland through Italy and France. His letters home were full of reactions to his piece on baptism, requests for reassurance that 'Ymadawiad Arthur' had been safely posted to Bangor and traveller's tales. He was convinced even before the word came that his expulsion was inevitable: 'Well, well! What is my future to be?' (*BBNA*, p. 105).

Dying now, and aware of it, Bowen burned his bridges. From on board the *SS Koenig*, he posted a second piece on free communion: 'The first article', he assured his brother with relish, 'is tame and mild in comparison' (Ibid., p. 125). A week later, whilst staying in Lisbon, he questioned the literal truth of the Resurrection, calling it 'more of a mystery than a fact for me' (Ibid., p. 138). The invalid who had dreamed of returning to Wales as a prophet with a message for his country now identified himself with Jeremiah. Although both pieces were hastily withdrawn once he reached Wales, they could not be unwritten, and nor could the larger work, 'Cymundeb Rhydd' (Free Communion), his unfinished *summa theologica*, found after his death.

In his contribution to Bowen's *Cofiant*, 'Blwyddyn Olaf Ben Bowen' (Ben Bowen's Final Year), his friend James James chose to ignore the controversy these pieces provoked:

> Our path leads us past the fields of heated and controversial debates gone by, where giants contested . . . but even though we are not 'entirely unversed' in these fields, we believe that it is more fitting and safer to 'pass by on the other side' away from these dangerous places, since we do not consider them essential to our task . . . (*CBBB*, p. lviii)

Better by far, he concluded, would be to allow the subject to dictate his own terms:

> Ben walked an untrodden road; he made a path for himself, and our intention will be to follow it as well as we may. We shall try to stay near Ben; and may Heaven aid us to be faithful to that child of genius . . . We are greatly tempted to become the oppressor of his oppressors; but were we to do so we would lose the society of Ben Bowen, even though he, in an unguarded hour, turned in that direction . . . We wish to do this with Ben's own broad and open spirit, remembering

that that we do so under the banner of One who is greater and finer – the Man of sorrows and acquainted with grief. (Ibid.)

Within a fortnight of his arrival home he had been expelled from Moriah. The committee seized on a technicality – that Bowen had been given a 'letter of release' from the church prior to his stay in South Africa – to argue that his membership no longer stood. Bowen appealed, but his request was ignored. Retrospectively, Moriah attempted to distance itself from him, claiming that his acceptance as a preacher had only been allowed 'under the law of tolerance . . . because of his great insistence and for fear that he would in the end come to embarrass the church' (Ibid., p. lxv).

Rumours abounded about his fondness for alcohol and billiards during his time in Kimberley. The press alluded to his mental instability. For a while, it became a parlour game in Welsh Baptist circles to guess which denomination would adopt him. T. T. Hughes, writing in *Seren Cymru* in June, weighed up the odds:

> He will not be accepted by the churches of England and Rome, because he is too critical of ritual. He will not be accepted by Wales's baptismal denominations, because he denies the scriptural basis of those things which they hold most dear. He cannot join the Salvation Army, because he would have to wail 'Come to Jesus' on some street corner, and there is no Jesus without the resurrection. Nothing remains for him but to found his own denomination, as other great men have done before him. What a strange denomination that would be! Communion would be denied to no one within it, member or no. If some wished to baptize their infants, Ben Bowen would be willing to do so, because although it is not scriptural, it is very beautiful, as are the Pope's robes. If someone wished to be baptized, the founder would be sympathetic enough to do so, even though it is 'a passive ritual'. And by the same token, of course, he could not refuse to circumcise the Israelites within his diocese. (Ibid., p. lxvi)

Criticism was something which Bowen relished; mockery was something new. By August he had become a Methodist, accepted as a member at Jerusalem, Ton. It was the chapel from which he was buried almost exactly a year later. He toyed with legal proceedings for slander, but friends dissuaded him.

September saw him at the Eisteddfod in Bangor (see p. 52), a spectator as the hitherto almost unknown Thomas Gwynn Jones, a Caernarfon journalist, was chaired for 'Ymadawiad Arthur'. Undeterred, Bowen stayed on in Caernarfonshire until the end of the month, working on the *awdl* topic for the following year's National Eisteddfod, 'Y Celt'. 'I feel like a little bird,' he wrote to Myfyr Hefin, 'healthier and stronger than I have been since I came back (*BBNA*, p. 177).'

It had been his ambition to spend the winter in the country, experimenting with the open-air treatment which was then fashionable for consumptives, but the weather in the north was so wet that he was forced to return home, staying until his death with his sister Mary at Ton Pentre, a mile or so from where he had been born. By February 1903 the haemorrhages which had been held in check in South Africa had recurred. Friends remarked on the young man they had known two years before, bent double, painfully thin and walking with a stick. Spring and summer that year were uncommonly wet. The infection spread to his kidneys. He became an invalid, composing what poetry he managed to produce in short bursts between long spells lying on a couch in the front room, where the door and the windows were left permanently open. His diet was the diet of the sanatorium he had so wanted to avoid.

He completed his last major work, 'Gardd Eden' (The Garden of Eden), on the first of May 1903, for the chair at that year's eisteddfod in Rhymni. Large in conception, its function was simple: a paradoxical embracing of lost innocence. Bowen could deny it:

> Nid llecyn bythwyrdd o dan ddwyfol wlith
> Yn deffro hiraeth y ddynoliaeth fyth
> I wylo am a fu yw Eden Ardd;
> Na! mae cyfrinach Duw yn fil mwy hardd . . . (*CBBB*, p. 234)

(The Garden of Eden is no evergreen spot
Sprinkled with divine dew
Making mankind long always for what was;
No! the the secret of God is a thousand times
    more beautiful . . .)

But the image of the garden, the retreat, is precisely that: a memory of what his own ambition and desire for knowledge had surrendered. The paradox of knowing innocence was founded on a still greater paradox. Bowen looked forward to a future which would restore the past. The gates to the garden, barred and guarded against man's inquisitiveness since the time of Adam's disobedience, would be reopened. The price for Eden restored would be a surrender of all intellectual aspiration. Bowen called it 'symledd Ysbrydoliaeth' ('the simplicity of Inspiration'): 'Man', he claimed, 'would walk in God's company as if in the company of Man' (Ibid.). In this respect, he distanced himself from Milton; his aim was not to justify the ways of God to man, but rather to explain the role of man within the divine pact:

> Mae dyn a Duw ynghyd, a'i gyfran gan
> Bob un; y dyn yn mynd ymlaen â'r gwaith,
> A Duw'r perchenog yma a thraw ar daith,
> yn d'od bob borau i gael ffrwyth ei ran!
>
> 'Ei ran,' – cyfiawnder! – y gyfrinach fawr
> Sy fyth rhwng Duw a dyn, a gwynfyd sydd
> Tu ol i'r cyfan, megis toriad dydd
> Tu ol i'r mynydd o fy mlaen yn awr. (Ibid., p. 235)

(Man and God together, and each one
With his portion; man carries out the work,
And God the owner travelling here and there,
Comes each morning to claim his share!

'His share,' – that's justice! – the great secret
Which is ever between God and man, and joy
lies behind the whole, like the break of day
Behind the mountain standing before me now.)

Under the pact, mankind becomes happy with its limitations: 'fel plentyn wrth ei fodd ar liniau'i dad' ('like a child delighted to sit on his father's knee') (Ibid., p. 236); his life lies 'nid mewn gwybod ond mwynhau' ('not in knowledge but in enjoyment') (Ibid.). The secret that Adam and Eve shared was a cloudless babyhood, soothed by God's lullaby. The pact was broken by a lust for knowledge. A few months before, these words would have been unthinkable from a young poet who considered doubt an earnest of faith and intellectual enquiry a moral obligation, who told his brother to cling to the ways of his parents but to allow him to pursue his own search for truth. Now, in what was a more autobiographical work than many of his readers would have guessed, he recanted:

> Dros lwybrau rhyddid sydd yn gwawdio deddf,
> A chwant sy'n gwerthu argyhoeddiad gwell,
> Drwy gyntedd brwnt uchelgais na faidd troed
> Cyfiawnder ddilyn fyth, fe ruthra'r dyn
> I gysegr gwybod sy'n anghofio'r Nef,
> At allor rheswm sydd yn gwrthod Duw,
> A'i Wynfa'n offrwm anghyfiawnder rhydd! (Ibid., p. 237)

> (Across the paths of freedom which mock the law,
> And a lust which betrays a better conviction,
> Through the filthy halls of an ambition
> Where the foot of justice would never dare follow, man rushes
> To the sanctuary of knowledge that forgets Heaven,
> To the altar of reason which refuses God,
> And his Paradise becomes an offering to unfettered injustice!)

Freedom was now equated with injustice, knowledge with guilt. Bowen, the dying returnee, more an exile now than he had been during his time in Africa, sought a way back:

> Adda – myfi – dynoliaeth – dal yr un
> Mae profiad chwerw'r oesau: rhaid i ddyn
> Blygu i ddeddf ei fyd, neu wyro i fedd;
> A pharchu hawliau Duw neu golli ei hedd ...

> Gwybod pob peth! – nid hawl dynoliaeth yw:
> Mae pren Gwybodaeth ar diriogaeth Duw;
> Mae rhyw ddirgelwch fyth â'i ddyeithr ffin
> Yn cadw Duw yn Dduw a dyn yn ddyn. (Ibid., pp. 240–1)

> (Adam – myself – mankind – the bitter experience
> Of the ages remains the same: man must
> Submit to the law of his world or bow to the grave;
> And respect the rights of God or surrender his peace.
>
> To know everything! – it is not mankind's right:
> The Tree of Knowledge is on God's estate;
> Some mystery always sets a strange boundary
> That keeps God as God, and man as man.)

Although he dressed it in the language of orthodoxy, in a sense, 'Gardd Eden' is a pre-Christian poem, an opportunity for Bowen to announce publicly his rejection of 'coegddysg ynfyd' ('absurd pseudo-learning'), and seek, as he had done throughout his adult life, to determine the conditions of his own salvation. At the same time, it is an attempt at reconciliation with the faith of his childhood and with the society he had left behind.

The poem was an exercise in intellectual self-destruction. It was mirrored by a corresponding physical decline. On the day it was posted, a further haemorrhage occurred. Bowen's final months were spent as a virtual invalid. In true Edwardian fashion, family and friends gathered around the deathbed, eager to catch the dying poet's last words. 'Do you know', Myfyr Hefin reported him as saying as the summer wore on, 'it is very odd if I am to go now; now that I feel secure, and now that I feel I have grasped the secret of poetry' (Ibid., p. lxxxviii).

Ben Bowen

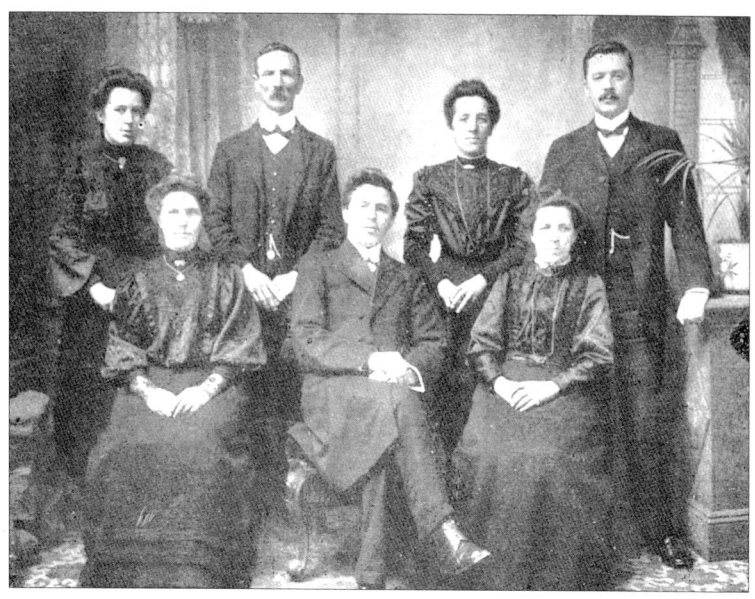

Ben Bowen's surviving brothers and sisters. David (Myfyr Hefin) stands far right; Mary is seated, left.

Epilogue

EVEN ALLOWING FOR THE IMPETUOSITY OF YOUTH, THERE WAS A restlessness in Ben Bowen which only death could ultimately resolve. His life had become a series of provisional escapes. He left the pit at the earliest opportunity, set his sights on the pulpit and then had second thoughts. He wanted the recognition of the eisteddfod but held those who controlled it in contempt. He toyed with the idea of writing in English, wanted to settle in South Africa, wanted to be a journalist, wanted to be a country postman, wanted to return to Wales, wanted a higher education, wanted to scandalize, wanted to die reconciled. Wishes and whims became confused. On his deathbed, with 400 lines of his last composition, 'Y Celt' for the National Eisteddfod in Llanelli, completed, he asked to be spared until the age of thirty. At thirty, he would doubtless have asked to live to see thirty-five. Gratification was always a few years away, a retreating horizon.

It is tempting to dismiss his lasting literary significance. He inspired no imitators, broke no new ground, and his verse is stubbornly unquotable. In death, at a hundred years' distance, he has mutated from wunderkind to mere oddity. His world is scarcely recognizable. The eisteddfod tradition, language and chapel culture of the Valleys which, between them, gave him a voice all but perished with him. The concerns which exercised him are dead ones. If he has any life at all, it is only to the extent that the serious men in beards and high collars who championed him and rejected him by turns seem deader still.

Even so, the gaunt, bright-eyed young Welshman who sat for the photographer in that Kimberley studio at the beginning of the twentieth century is a compelling figure. Our past, or the past which we know about at a generation or two's remove, is the future he never saw. All the things which he might have been expected to witness as a mature man are about to be taken from him. The camera captures him ignorant of two world wars, the death of empire and the irreversible change of the industry and the society which bred him. Aware of his own impending death, he looks forward, rather, to two hopes of immortality: literary renown on the one hand, and, on the other, the life everlasting promised to all the saints. He died still hopeful of both but convinced of neither. If the twentieth century needs a metaphor, perhaps it is this photograph.

Bibliographical Note

No full-length study of Ben Bowen's work exists, in Welsh or English, and all his published work is long out of print. For a brief guide to his life, in English, see Meic Stephens (ed.), *The New Companion to the Literature of Wales* (Cardiff, 1998), p. 62, and Ben Bowen Thomas's contribution to *The Dictionary of Welsh Biography down to 1940* (Cardiff, 1959), p. 46.

In preparing this work I drew upon Cennard Davies's chapter, 'O olwg hagrwch Cynnydd: golwg ar farddoniaeth Ben Bowen', in Hywel Teifi Edwards (ed.), *Cwm Rhondda* (Llandysul, 1995), and on Ben Bowen's own posthumous works, edited by his brother Myfyr Hefin: *Cofiant a Barddoniaeth Ben Bowen* (*CBBB*) (Caerdydd, 1904), *Rhyddiaith Ben Bowen* (*RhBB*) (Caerdydd, 1909) and *Ben Bowen yn Neheudir Affrica* (*BBNA*) (Caerdydd, 1928). I also consulted Ben Bowen's academic papers, held in his brother's archive at the National Library of Wales. The other two volumes cited in the text, *Blagur Awen Ben Bowen* (Caernarfon, 1915) and *Ben Bowen i'r Ieuanc* (Llanelli, 1928) are selections from the three main volumes named above.

A picture of his birthplace and memorial can be seen at http://www.bbc.co.uk/cymru/lleisiaulleol/deddwyrain/y_gloran/hanes.shtml

Index

Note: page references in italic refer to illustrations.

Bardd Newydd 23–4, 27–8, 43, 56–7
Ben Bowen i'r Ieuanc 3
Ben Bowen yn Neheudir Affrica 3
Blagur Awen Ben Bowen 3
Boer War 37, 54, 57–8
Bowen, Ann (sister) 40, *66*
Bowen, Ben
 birth 8; childhood 9–10, *11*; health 19, 36–7, 40, 51, 60, 62, 65; as a miner 11–13, 54; spirituality 11–13, 16–17, 19, 30–2, 34–5, 37–40, 47, 51, 63–5; critical reputation 7, 21–4, 26, 29–30, 48, 67–8; education 14–15, *18*, 19; physical appearance 2
 major works:
 'Adgofion' 25–6; *Durtur y Deffro* 15; 'Gardd Eden' 33, 62–5; 'Goleuni y Byd' 49–51, 58; 'Y Deffroad Cenedlaethol' 13, 27–9; 'Y Diwygiwr' 36, 42–9, 50, 54; 'Williams Pantycelyn' 19, 42; 'Y Celt' 67; 'Ymadawiad Arthur' 54–7, 58, 60
 funeral 3–4
 memorial service 4, 6
Bowen, David (brother) see Myfyr Hefin
Bowen, Dinah (mother) 8
Bowen, Mary (sister) 19, 62, *66*
Bowen, Thomas (father) 8, 9, *11*, 13, 19
Cape Town 20, 21, 33, 36–7, 55
Cofiant a Barddoniaeth Ben Bowen 3, 9–10

Cymru (O. M. Edwards) 5, 35
Cymru Fydd 26
Cymru'r Plant (O. M. Edwards) 35
Edwards, O. M. 5, 13, 35
Eisteddfod, National 1, 12, 14, 19, 22–3, 36, *52*, 54–5, 62, 67
Ellis, Thomas Edward 1
Gruffydd, W. J. 21
Harris, Hywel 28
Hedd Wyn 1
Heddyw (O. M. Edwards) 13–14
Jones, Thomas Gwynn 21–2, 44, 55–6
Kimberley 1, 37, *41*, 57, 61, 67
Lloyd George, David 1
Morgan, Eluned 6
Morris-Jones, John 22
Myfyr Hefin 2, 3, 5, 9, 10, 12, 29, 35–6, 39, 40, 47–9, 51, 54, 65, *66*
Owen, Daniel 28
Parry, R. Williams 21
Parry, Thomas 23
Rhondda Valley 4–5, 8–9, 12, 13, 19, 26
Rhyddiaith Ben Bowen 3
Roberts, Silyn 21
Rowland, Daniel 28
South Africa 1, 19–20, 33, 35, 37, 40, 57–9, 61, 67
Thomas, Ben Bowen 3
Treorci 8–9, 12–13, 37
Yr Ysgol Farddol (Dafydd Morganwg) 10